OCCASIONAL PAPER 197

Deposit Insurance
Actual and Good Practices

Gillian G.H. Garcia

INTERNATIONAL MONETARY FUND
Washington DC
2000

Production: IMF Graphics Section
Figures: Sanaa Elaroussi
Typesetting: Choon Lee

Library of Congress Cataloging-in-Publication Data

Garcia, G. G.
  Deposit insurance : actual and good practices / Gillian G. H. Garcia.
    p. cm. — (Occasional paper ; 197)
  Includeds bibliographical references.
  ISBN 1-55775-948-0
    1. Deposit Insurance.   I. Title.   II. Occasional paper (International
Monetary Fund) ; no. 197.

HG1662.A3 G37 2000
368.8′54′00973—dc21   00-063356

Price: US$20.00
(US$17.00 to full-time faculty members and
students at universities and colleges)

Please send orders to:
International Monetary Fund, Publication Services
700 19th Street, N.W., Washington, D.C. 20431, U.S.A.
Tel.: (202) 623-7430   Telefax: (202) 623-7201
E-mail: publications@imf.org
Internet: http://www.imf.org

recycled paper

Contents

The following symbols have been used throughout this paper:

. . .   to indicate that data are not available;

n.a.   to indicate not applicable;

—   to indicate that the figure is zero or less than half the final digit shown, or that the item does not exist;

–   between years or months (i.e., 1997–98 or January–June) to indicate the years or months covered, including the beginning and ending years or months;

/   between years or months (i.e., 1997/98) to indicate a crop or fiscal (financial) year.

"Billion" means a thousand million; "trillion" means a thousand billion.

Minor discrepancies between constituent figures and totals are due to rounding.

The term "country," as used in this paper, does not in all cases refer to a territorial entity that is a state as understood by international law and practice; the term also covers some territorial entities that are not states, but for which statistical data are maintained and provided internationally on a separate and independent basis.

Preface

This paper is the culmination of several years of work by the IMF on deposit insurance—a subject that has grown increasingly important in recent years. During the 1980s and early 1990s, the IMF staff, including McCarthy (1980), Galbis (1988), Fries (1990), Fries and Peraudin (1991), and Garcia (1996), examined the analytical underpinning of deposit protection. With the emergence of the transition economies in Central and Eastern Europe, the IMF focused on the introduction of deposit insurance in countries with diverse financial structures and different macroeconomic conditions. Requests from the transition countries prompted a search for good practices. In response, the IMF conducted a series of surveys of country practices, which were shared with all members of the IMF. Notable among these studies were Kyei (1995) and Lindgren and Garcia (1996).

During the mid- and late 1990s, a number of countries considered introducing deposit protection systems as a means of stabilizing their banking systems and protecting depositors from loss, and they sought advice from the IMF in this effort. The IMF generally has cautioned countries about such moves, arguing that appropriate political, institutional, and economic preconditions needed to be in place before deposit protection could be effective.

Given the continued requests from members for advice on depositor protection, IMF management called for the development of operational definitions of best practices on depositor protection to ensure that the IMF staff were providing consistent advice. This led to the 1996 operational paper, "Deposit Insurance and Crisis Management" by Carl-Johan Lindgren and Gillian Garcia. The paper was updated for presentation at the International Conference on Deposit Insurance arranged by the United States Federal Deposit Insurance Corporation in September 1998. This conference marked the first time deposit insurers from around the world convened to exchange views and experiences. The search for improved policies, standards, and practices led to the formation of a Study Group on Deposit Insurance under the auspices of the Financial Stability Forum (FSF). The study group recently issued its report and the search for an international consensus on deposit insurance designs and practices will be continued by a working group. The IMF is participating in this work of the stability forum.

The IMF staff has gained substantial experience regarding the benefits and pitfalls of deposit insurance systems and the preconditions for their success. Recent financial crises have also shown their limitations. The experiences of IMF staff in designing effective and incentive-compatible systems of deposit protection, and in the role of limited or full guarantees in resolving financial crises, are summarized in this Occasional Paper, which we hope will make a contribution to the international debate on the subject.

The author thanks Stanley Fischer, V. Sundararajan, Carl-Johan Lindgren, Charles Enoch, David Hoelscher, Michael Taylor, and participants in seminars sponsored by the IMF's Monetary and Exchange Affairs Department for insightful comments; country authorities and staff from the IMF and the World Bank who have responded to her inquiries; Elena Budreckaite for expert research assistance; and the staff assistants, particularly Funke Orimoloye, Lidia Tokuda, and Constanze Schulz-Calle La Rosa, who have typed and retyped this material. The work has benefited from the editorial expertise of Jeff Hayden of the External Relations Department, who also coordinated its publication.

I Overview

In most countries, banks are the most important financial institutions for intermediating between savers and borrowers, assessing risks, executing monetary policy, and providing payment services. At the same time, the configuration of their portfolios makes them especially vulnerable to illiquidity and insolvency. In particular, by law, bank deposits have to be repaid at par; in addition, banks are highly leveraged and often maintain liquid assets to meet withdrawals only in normal times. In light of this vulnerability, government officials realize that the demise of one bank, if handled poorly, can spill over to others, creating negative externalities and causing a more general problem for other banks in the system. For these reasons, many governments provide a safety net for banks that generally includes deposit protection and lender-of-last-resort facilities, in addition to a system of bank regulation and supervision. Recognizing that financial stability is a public good with regional, and even global, implications (see Wyplosz, 1999), the international community is showing an interest in deposit protection.

Although for many years the IMF and other international financial institutions have responded to inquiries from member countries concerning deposit insurance, their interest in the subject has intensified recently. Aided by the IMF's advantage of near universal membership (currently 182 countries), Kyei (1995) conducted a survey of both implicit and explicit systems of deposit insurance that were in existence in the early 1990s. Lindgren and Garcia (1996) surveyed explicit systems and detailed good practices for deposit insurance systems, while Garcia (1997b) and Folkerts-Landau and Lindgren (1998) summarized them. The World Bank's research includes that of Talley and Mas (1990) and recent papers by Demirguc-Kunt and Detragiache (1998 and 2000), Demirguc-Kunt and Huizinga (1999), and Honohan and Klingebiel (2000). The Financial Stability Forum has focused on deposit insurance in an effort to build an international consensus on best practices to discourage financial crises.

A country faces six choices regarding deposit protection: (1) an explicit denial of protection, as in New Zealand; (2) legal priority for the claims of depositors over other claimants during the liquidation of a failed bank, as in Hong Kong SAR, instead of a deposit guarantee; (3) ambiguity regarding coverage; (4) an implicit guarantee, as found in 55 countries by Kyei in 1995; (5) explicit limited coverage—in this paper in 67 countries; and (6) a full explicit guarantee, as exists currently in nine countries. Choosing the first or second option is legitimate, but rare. The sixth possibility is generally reserved for periods of severe and systemic crisis. This paper explores options five and six.

Much of the conceptual work on deposit protection has focused on the disadvantages of adopting explicit protection, whether limited or comprehensive. But these disadvantages may not be inevitable. Consequently, Section II of this paper explores ways to obtain the benefits of deposit insurance that so many countries seek while avoiding the well-explored pitfalls—moral hazard, adverse selection, and agency problems.[1] In doing so it presents a set of good practices for explicit limited deposit protection. It does so in the belief that explicit limited coverage, if well designed, is preferable to ambiguity and implicit coverage and that it can complement legal priority. Section III describes the actual configuration of 67 explicit, limited systems of deposit insurance known to be in operation in the year 2000. It will conclude with an assessment of recent movements toward good practice. Section IV shifts to a consideration of whether and when to institute full or "blanket" coverage, and when and how to remove it. Section V summarizes and concludes.

---

[1]Moral hazard occurs when protection causes the beneficiaries of insurance (in the case of deposit insurance, this means depositors, bank owners, managers and supervisors, and even politicians) to be careless in their approach to bank soundness. Adverse selection occurs when only the worst risks seek to take advantage of protection, resulting in a financially nonviable system. Agency problems occur when the agent does not execute the desires/commands of his/her principal. In deposit insurance, the problem occurs principally when supervisors and regulators put the interests of the industry they regulate above those of the general population ("regulatory capture") and when politicians interfere in the supervisor's performance of his/her public responsibilities, often at the taxpayer's expense.

II Good Practices for Deposit Insurance

The proliferation of banking and financial crises during the 1980s and 1990s has led a large number of countries to institute, or consider instituting, an explicit system of deposit insurance (see, for example, Lindgren, Garcia, and Saal, 1996).[2] In fact, 30 of the 72 countries now known to have an explicit deposit insurance system established it during the past decade; 49 set up their systems in the past 20 years. During the 1990s, 33 countries reformed their deposit insurance systems, often to improve its incentive structure in light of experience.[3]

Countries often have several objectives when they establish a deposit insurance system. Some of these objectives are achievable; others are not. One of the most common goals is to avoid an imminent systemic crisis or resolve an existing one; but this objective is regrettably unrealistic. The incompatibility arises because achieving it will, most probably, require a full guarantee, which conflicts with the incentives needed to keep the banking system sound in the long run. This part of the paper discusses deposit insurance systems only in normal times. As discussed in Section IV, a separate response may be needed to manage a contagious, systemic crisis, which may require overriding an existing deposit insurance system. Thus, an attempt to replace a full implicit guarantee by a limited deposit insurance system when the banking system is confronting significant problems is likely to be ineffective. Deposit insurance system initiation must wait until after the banking system has been recapitalized and restructured.

Under the deposit insurance system option, national regulators rely on both discipline from the markets and prudential regulation and supervision, including surveillance over the payment system, to counter the incentive problems and excessive risk taking that accompany deposit insurance. They use the lender of last resort to deal with liquidity problems of solvent banks and counter possible runs by large, informed depositors. (The lender of last resort confronts a practical problem, however. Typically, an insured bank can remain liquid long after it becomes insolvent and the central bank has difficulty in distinguishing illiquid but solvent banks from those that are both illiquid and insolvent.) The authorities also need to require data disclosure to the public in order to help depositors and other creditors exercise market discipline on banks. They enforce standards for adequate bank capitalization to avoid insolvencies, maintain other regulatory standards to assure good governance, limit excessive risk taking, and enforce firm entry and exit rules to keep the system sound.

As Table 1 suggests, it is essential to design an incentive-compatible system that discourages the pitfalls of deposit insurance—moral hazard, adverse selection, and agency problems. That will necessitate having appropriate objectives for the deposit insurance system, carefully construed roles and responsibilities for it, and a supportive infrastructure that ensures good internal and external governance for insured institutions. In implementation, the components of this framework will vary from country to country.

Objectives

Countries implement deposit insurance systems for a number of reasons. As Garcia (1996) discusses in more detail, these reasons include: (1) providing consumer protection for small depositors by providing a mechanism for the immediate pay-out or transfer of the insured portion of their deposits; (2) enhancing public confidence and systemic stability by establishing a framework for the resolution of failed banks that deals sternly and expeditiously with individual bank failures and so prevents them from spreading; (3) increasing savings and encouraging economic growth; (4) enabling small and new banks to compete with large and/or state-owned banks; (5) defining the boundaries of the government's expo-

---

[2]Sections II and III discuss systems of limited deposit insurance suitable for normal times. Section IV pertains to full (blanket) coverage offered during a systemic crisis.

[3]Many in the European Union and Eastern Europe did so to conform with the European Union's 1994 Directive on Deposit Guarantee Schemes.

Table 1. Good Practices for Deposit Insurance

Issue	Good Practice	Departures from Good Practice	Practical Issues to Be Resolved
Infrastructure	1. Have realistic objectives.	Expect deposit insurance system to avoid/resolve crises and subsidize favored industries.	Convincing politicians and the public about what is feasible and what is not.
	2. Choose carefully between a public or private deposit insurance system.	A publicly funded system that is privately run.	Who will finance and operate the system?
	3. Define the deposit insurance agency's mandate accordingly.	Pretending the system is private when it has public backing.	Coordinating with existing institutions; finding staff with integrity and skills.
	4. Have a good legal, judicial, accounting, financial, and political infrastructure.	Weak valuation, poor laws on collateral, bankruptcy, private property, a weak court system.	Which structures are best? How to put them into law and regulation and how to get them implemented. Which are the priority items?
Moral Hazard	5. Define the system explicitly in law and regulation. Conduct a public awareness campaign.	The system is implicit and ambiguous.	How to amend the laws and regulations to ensure transparency and certainty.
	6. Give the supervisor a system of prompt remedial actions.	The supervisor takes no, or late remedial actions.	Should these remedial powers be mandatory or discretionary?
	7. Resolve failed depository institutions promptly.	Ill-considered capital forbearance.	The types and importance of closure policies. Should the deposit insurance agency be involved?
	8. Provide low coverage.	There is high, even full coverage, which can impose an excessive fiscal burden and fosters moral hazard.	Which deposits should be covered, at what level; should there be coinsurance?
	9. Net (offset) loans in default against deposits.	Cover the deposits of borrowers in default.	Insuring the deposits of borrowers whose loans are current.
Adverse Selection	10. Make membership compulsory.	The scheme is voluntary.	Which classes of depository institutions should the deposit insurance system cover?
	11. Risk-adjust premiums, once the deposit insurance system has sufficient experience.	Flat rate premiums.	How best to set premiums according to risk?
Agency Problems	12. Create an independent but accountable deposit insurance system agency.	Political interference, lack of accountability.	Designing the deposit insurance agency and its board of directors (to avoid political interference but promote accountability).
	13. Have bankers on an advisory board, not the main board of a publicly run deposit insurance system with access to financial support from the government.	Bankers are in control, regulatory capture.	How best to avoid conflicts of interest?
	14. Ensure close relations with the lender of last resort and the supervisor.	Relationships are weak even contentious.	Poor lender-of-last-resort policies that raise costs to the deposit insurance system; how to share information.
Financial Integrity and Credibility	15. Start when banks are sound.	Start before resolving failed banks.	Identifying and preparing for the right time.
	16. Ensure adequate sources of funding (ex ante or ex post) to avoid insolvency.	The deposit insurance system is under-funded or insolvent, and makes demands on the budget.	What are the appropriate levels for premiums and the accumulated fund? Should depositors have legal priority over the assets of a failed bank?
	17. Invest fund resources wisely.	Invest in risky assets, such as deposits in problem banks.	Whether to invest in domestic or foreign government securities.
	18. Pay out or transfer deposits quickly.	There are delays in payment.	How to effect prompt payment?

Table 1 *(concluded)*

Issue	Good Practice	Departures from Good Practice	Practical Issues to Be Resolved
Financial Integrity and Credibility *(concluded)*	19. Organize good information on the condition of individual institutions and the distribution of deposits by size.	Have bad information based on poor accounting, valuation, loan classification and provisioning standards, and no data on the distribution of deposits by size.	What other data do supervisors and the deposit insurance system need? How to share data effectively?
	20. Make appropriate disclosure to maintain confidence while enabling depositors to protect their interest.	Make little, or misleading disclosure, and a discredited press.	What should be disclosed and when?

Note: These good practices are applicable in normal times. Good practices during systemic crises are described in Section IV.
Sources: Developed from Folkerts-Landau, Lindgren, and others (1998) and Garcia (1999, 2000).

sure to loss when a bank or group of banks fail in normal times; and (6) requiring banks to contribute to the resolution of failed peers. In sum, protecting small depositors and enhancing stability by strengthening the incentive structure, which includes a strong exit framework, should be the principal reasons for adopting a deposit insurance system.

Most countries, including those that are members of the European Union, emphasize small-depositor (consumer) protection as the main objective of their deposit insurance system. A system could be expected to cope with isolated and even multiple bank failures, if the deposits involved comprise a reasonably small percentage of total system deposits.[4] A properly designed scheme can help to eliminate self-justifying runs by small depositors and so contribute to the overall stability of deposits and the banking system. Moreover, a stable pool of small, core deposits enhances a bank's franchise value and so facilitates the timely and orderly resolution of weak banks, which serves to keep the banking system efficient. In this way, deposit insurance can also establish a more rational system for forcing the closure with restructuring, rather than the liquidation, of nonviable banks. A deposit insurance system also promotes competition in that it assists small banks to compete with larger banks that may be deemed "too big to fail."

The first principle suggests that all depository institutions, including commercial, investment, merchant, savings, cooperative banks, finance companies, and credit unions that offer par valued deposits to the public, should be covered by deposit insurance.[5] The deposit insurance system will need to provide incentives to contain the pitfalls of deposit insurance—moral hazard, adverse selection, and agency problems. And insured banks will need close supervision to bolster the incentive structure.

However, countries often harbor unrealistic expectations for deposit insurance. It is not an appropriate vehicle for providing preferences to politically favored industries—that is a fiscal responsibility. Moreover, the elimination of runs on all categories of deposits is not a viable objective for deposit insurance. Limited coverage will not protect large, wholesale, or interbank deposits (both domestic and foreign), which are the deposits most prone to runs. Once a systemic crisis develops, limited-coverage deposit insurance will not protect the large-value payment system nor prevent a flight to quality, flight abroad, or the collapse of the system. Thus, *a well-designed deposit insurance system can be, at best, just one component of a sound financial system.*

The Deposit Insurance System's Mandate: Public or Private

A privately run scheme will benefit from peer pressure to keep the system sound and avoid costs to

---

[4]The Bank Insurance Fund in the United States successfully resolved 1,394 failed banks between 1984 and 1992. The assets of these failed banks represented 10 percent of all insured bank assets in 1984 and 6.6 percent in 1992.

[5]For a definition of the term, "deposit," and a discussion of the characteristics of depository institutions that make them candidates for protection, see Garcia (1996), which also discusses other objectives for deposit protection, including increasing competition and promoting economic growth, that countries sometimes harbor for their insurance system.

members, but it may not be able to cope with widespread failures. In turn, the choice between a public and a private system will influence the scope of the deposit insurance agency's functions.

There are two legitimate and contrasting models governing the ownership of the deposit insurance system under normal conditions. Both are already in existence around the world. One is privately run and entirely privately funded, and the other is government-backed and run. Argentina has a privately funded and privately run system. The United States has a government-run system that is privately funded but has explicit government backing. (There are also instances of privately funded and privately run insurance systems that have, usually informal, government backing; but these are likely to give rise to conflicts of interest.) While the private deposit insurance agency could have a limited agenda, a government-run insurance agency could have wider roles and responsibilities.

The deposit insurance system will be successful only if it is financially viable and has earned the public's confidence. There also should be clear understanding as to who will back up the system if it should become insolvent or illiquid, and under what circumstances support will be provided. When banking problems are severe, the system will, most probably, need government backing. A privately run system may lack credibility without such government support. But if it has that support, it may be tempted to set premiums too low for financial self-sufficiency under the assurance that the government will cover the financial gap. For this reason, the deposit insurance system in many countries will need to be run by a government agency to protect the public interest and the taxpayer from loss.[6] Regardless of who runs the system, it will need a good legal framework, as discussed below.

The System's Mandate: Narrow or Broad?

A deposit insurance system can embrace a wide range of responsibilities, but fundamentally its mandate may be either narrow or broad. It is important to establish a clear understanding of the role and responsibilities of the deposit insurance agency or authority so that it can fulfill its obligations effectively and adopt an appropriate organizational structure. This understanding, especially where membership in the insurance system is limited, allows for modest staffing.

The Narrow Mandate

A narrow system may be merely a "paybox" that compensates insured depositors of failed banks. Its principal responsibility will be to:
- Insure small depositors in member institutions. Doing so will involve verifying depositors' claims and paying out or transferring deposits to another bank when called upon to do so by the supervisory authority.
- Compensate insured depositors in failed member institutions promptly to minimize disruption to the economy. Delaying payment/transfer diminishes the value of the guarantee and dishonors public trust.

Additional responsibilities include:
- Setting and collecting premiums. Premiums can be assessed quarterly or semiannually based on the reports banks submit to their supervisors. Setting premiums is discussed later.
- Managing the insurance fund in a way that allows it to satisfy its obligations effectively, keep insurance premiums low to protect member institutions' interests, and maintain the soundness of the banking industry. This implies that the fund's resources be invested in safe assets. (See the section "Promoting Credibility.")
- Informing the public of its role and responsibilities and describing how it works.

Once the bank is intervened or placed in receivership/liquidation, ownership of deposits should be verified and the amount that is covered in full should be made available rapidly.[7] A well-prepared deposit insurance agency can make (full or partial) payment over the weekend when a bank is closed on a Friday, but certainly within 30 days. Compensation can be made in a number of ways. Paying out deposits in cash should be avoided, if possible. Where payouts have to be made, however, payment through automatic teller machines (ATMs) can be an efficient option. A preferred option is to transfer insured deposits from an intervened bank to another institution that is willing to take them and even to pay a premium to receive them (along with a negotiated amount of the failed banks' or other assets). The recipient bank will make the insured deposits available to their owners by opening accounts for them, or provide a refund in person or by mail. Regardless of the method, the funds should be accessible within one or two days to protect the payment system and to avoid runs on other banks by small depositors, for whom it is not cost effective to evaluate the safety of

---

[6]The government in Argentina has attempted to overcome the problem of a privately run deposit insurance system setting low premiums by establishing a legal target size for the system's fund.

[7]An intervened bank is one that has deteriorated so far that the supervisors take control temporarily or permanently from its owners and managers.

their bank, even if they have the sophistication and information to do so.[8]

Supervisory authorities sometimes need to suspend deposit withdrawals. While they should seek to avoid suspension or limits on the amount that can be withdrawn, authorities may need to use such measures to permit valuation and loss-sharing. In such cases, the restrictions should apply only to large deposits. Small depositors should retain access to limited amounts of their funds. Moreover, the suspension should stay in place for the shortest possible time.

In setting up the relationship between the supervisor and the deposit insurance system, policymakers should take the following into account:

- Deposit insurance agency staff in a privately or jointly run agency must analyze information received from the supervisory authority and elsewhere to protect the insurance fund. Clear lines of communication between the agency and the supervisor need to be worked out, since the agency must be aware of which individual institutions could pose a risk to the insurance fund. All information and decisions pertaining to banks gathered by the agency must be classified as strictly confidential, and agency staff should be subject to the same confidentiality rules as supervisors. Providing information to bankers in a privately run deposit guarantee is, therefore, a problem.
- The deposit insurance agency must communicate its concerns over problem banks to the supervisor. Initially the agency could express its concerns verbally. Later, it should do so in a formal written communication to the head of the supervisory agency. Subsequently, if no action or inadequate action has been taken by supervisor, in a publicly backed scheme, the agency must notify an appropriate government agency of its concerns. This agency will often be the ministry of finance, because it is the ministry that will ultimately have to meet any deficiency in the system's funds.

The ultimate in a narrowly defined deposit insurance agency would be one that is a separate legal entity in concept only. It could delegate some or all of its responsibilities to the central bank, the bank supervisor, or to the ministry of finance.

The Broad Mandate

Under a broader construction, the deposit insurance agency may also:

- Monitor the condition of the banking industry to estimate its potential losses and take actions to minimize or forestall those losses.
- Take responsibility for the resolution of insured financial institutions that have been intervened by the supervisory authority. Institutions should remain the responsibility of the supervisor until they have been intervened. Under the supervisor's authority, they will be subject to a range of corrective measures, including statutory prompt corrective action, whereby the supervisor may take temporary control of the institution and install new management. Once the supervisor has intervened in an institution and taken it permanently from its owners, responsibility for it should immediately pass to the deposit insurance agency.

Apart from compensating insured depositors promptly, the broadly defined agency has a fiduciary responsibility to avoid losses and to obtain as much as possible for the failed bank's portfolio. A more detailed discussion is beyond the scope of this paper, but it may be possible to merge an entire failed entity into another institution, or to pass a negotiated portion of assets to another bank together with the insured deposits in a purchase and assumption transaction. Otherwise, it may be necessary to liquidate the assets in full or in part. Resolution powers should be granted to the agency by law, and it should use a combination of methods of resolution that is least costly to it (on the basis of discounted present value over a relevant time horizon).

In a systemic crisis, however, a special agency may have to be established to cope with a flood of insolvencies and the disposal of a large volume of assets from failed banks.[9] While the deposit insurance authority also could be assigned such additional functions as restructuring and liquidating banks, these aspects go beyond the topic of depositor protection and are not covered in this paper. However, these additional powers need to be clearly anchored in the law.

Infrastructure

Both public and private deposit insurance systems need to be supported by a strong infrastructure of civil and commercial law to strengthen property

---

[8]The deposit insurance systems of Argentina in 1982 and Venezuela in 1994 did not pay insured deposits promptly. This omission had severe repercussions on depositor confidence.

[9]While the Federal Deposit Insurance Corporation (FDIC) was successful in handling the large number of bank failures that occurred in the late 1980s and early 1990s in the United States, the Federal Savings and Loan Insurance Corporation (FSLIC) was not. It was abolished and a temporary agency, the Resolution Trust Corporation (1989–1995), was created to handle a similarly large number of failed thrift institutions.

rights. A clear understanding of their fiduciary responsibilities by bank owners and managers will enhance internal governance. Internationally accepted accounting and auditing standards will facilitate realistic loan valuations and empower market discipline. Public disclosure of individual bank data will also encourage market discipline.[10] The system also needs to be supported by a well-formulated lender of last resort and adequate risk-management framework in the payment system. These and other relevant topics are beyond the scope of this paper, but attention will be given to supervision and regulation, which need to be buttressed to make the deposit guarantee successful.

Supervision, Regulation, and Resolution

The regulatory and supervisory system should require fit-and-proper owners and operators, enforce rules for governance and capitalization, limit risk taking, require information disclosure to the public as well as the supervisor, and execute a set of prompt corrective actions to forestall and, if necessary, swiftly resolve insolvencies (see Folkerts-Landau and Lindgren, 1998).

The supervisory authorities should force the strict resolution of problem banks, using a swift application of a spectrum of enforcement actions to be taken as soon as a bank becomes undercapitalized or shows other signs of weakness. The objective is to turn the weak bank around toward recovery before it becomes nonviable and places burdens on the deposit insurance system. A system of prompt corrective actions, sometimes also called structured early intervention and resolution (SEIR), is a key component of an efficient and competitive banking system.[11]

Requiring and enforcing capital requirements also protect the deposit insurance system. They serve a similar purpose to that of a high deductible in property and casualty insurance in making the insured party reluctant to take excessive risks. In addition, preventing undercapitalized banks from paying dividends or making side payments to their owners and managers will make it more difficult for these parties to loot the bank (Akerlof and Romer, 1993). While restricting the insured bank to holding only safe assets (narrow banking) or collateralizing insured deposits with relatively risk-free assets will also serve to diminish the number of bank failures and the cost to the insurance fund of resolving those

that do occur, narrow banking has practical limitations and foregoes many of the natural synergies of banking. (Further discussion of narrow banking lies beyond the scope of this paper).

Prompt corrective action/SEIR should allow supervisors to intervene in a problem bank *before* it becomes book-value insolvent and provide the basis for the prompt closure of the bank should it become necessary.[12] Almost universally, experience has shown that an onsite examination or external audit of a bank that is approaching book-value insolvency reveals that the provisions for loan losses are inadequate. Thus, such a bank is, in fact, already insolvent at current market value—and often deeply so—and will be found to be insolvent at book value once a proper asset valuation is made. Delay in closure almost always deepens the costs of a bank's insolvency, partly because owners can abuse the deposit insurance system, loot the bank, and/or gamble for recovery with those deposit funds that remain in place and with new deposits that are attracted by higher interest rates and the fact that they are guaranteed.

Instead of delay, the supervisor, or the deposit insurer when it has a broad mandate, needs a strong framework for the resolution of failed banks that encourages the owners and managers of each bank to keep their bank strong and retain control over it. The supervisor needs authority to close and liquidate or resolve insolvent banks in some other incentive-compatible manner.

Supervisors often express a preference for exercising regulatory discretion in disciplining or closing a problem bank. Yet, having discretion exposes supervisors to political interference, and experience has shown that they may be pressured to use that discretion inadvisably to postpone corrective actions. The optimal balance between rules and discretion will vary from country to country according to local conditions, such as the efficiency of the legal system, strength of the civil service, and political tradition.

Requiring Subordinated Debt

Subordinated debt—debt that ranks behind other non-equity claims in a liquidation—has a dual role in strengthening the banking system. As an addition to the bank's equity capital, it acts both as a buffer against losses and a market signal of bank condition. As a junior debt, or quasi-equity, subordinated debt can be written down more easily than deposits or unsubordinated credits. The subordinated debt contract

---

[10]Realistic loan valuation requires effective regulation and supervision of loan classification and provisioning.

[11]See Benston and Kaufman (1988) for an early exposition of prompt corrective actions/SEIR.

[12]U.S. law, for example, requires supervisors to intervene and pass the troubled bank to the FDIC, when its leverage ratio falls below 2 percent.

should make clear to holders their exposure to loss in the situation where the bank is closed.

This useful function has led a number of regulators and economists to advocate an increased role for subordinated debt in the capital structure of large publicly traded banks.[13] Under such proposals, large banks at all times should be required to issue subordinated debt that has been rated by an acceptable rating agency equivalent to, at least, 2 percent of their assets. Some of this debt should be short term, so that the bank needs to reissue its subordinated debt frequently. The ease or difficulty of the issuance process and the contractual terms of the issue will give the bank's supervisors additional information on the markets' perceptions of the bank's condition. Moreover, this capital would be exposed to loss sharing.[14]

Subordinated debt is not a substitute for a deposit insurance system, but it could be a useful complement. Requiring subordinated debt is feasible only for large publicly traded banks, and issuance of such debt would be difficult, even for large banks, in undeveloped markets. In Argentina, which appears to be one of the few countries to have set a subordinated debt requirement to date, critics argue that the market is thin, with virtually no secondary market, and that bank owners can rig the market by buying the debt.[15] Canada has considered, but not adopted, a proposal to require subordinated debt.

A Framework For Resolving Individual Banks

All countries need a firm framework for the resolution of troubled banks. If it does not already exist, the establishment of a system of deposit insurance provides an opportunity to design and enact a legal and institutional framework that will help authorities to intervene in, sell, or close troubled banks—in whole or in part. Such a clear legal framework will foster early action in the resolution of problem banks and will help to avoid costly delays, thus expanding the opportunities for the resolution of individual banks to keep the financial system sound. However, there is a need to make certain that the legal framework for the deposit insurance system is also adequately reflected in the banking law, and that it does not conflict with other laws (e.g., company law, the code of commercial and personal bankruptcy, etc.).

In the case of a broad mandate, the resolution framework should require that the bank pass to the government-run deposit insurance agency for resolution immediately after it has been intervened by the supervisory authority. The agency would then compensate insured depositors, write down shareholders' equity, and impose losses ("haircuts") on uninsured depositors and unsecured creditors. The power to do so would be granted to the agency by law. The agency would seek to merge a failed bank with another bank, conduct a purchase and assumption transaction, oversee a liquidation, or combine any of these actions with the aim of minimizing its own cost, but it would have no authority to provide open bank assistance, for example, by infusing liquidity or providing capital to a bank that has not been intervened. The problem with open bank assistance is that it can be too easily abused to bail out owners.

Too Big to Fail

Country authorities and markets frequently consider some banks to be "too big to fail," that is, too big to be closed and liquidated.[16] There are arguments for and against such a policy. On the one hand, the too-big-to-fail argument tends to be excessively invoked by authorities as an excuse for not taking failed banks from their owners—often for political reasons. On the other hand, many banking systems are heavily concentrated and the closure and liquidation of a bank representing, say, more than 10–20 percent of a banking system's assets could have major systemic implications.[17] As long as the owners and managers of a failed bank are not bailed out and there is an operational and financial restructuring to restore viability to the bank, a too-big-to-fail policy means that the state saves the economic infrastructure of the bank, absorbs the losses, and often assumes ownership temporarily until reprivatization (see Enoch, Garcia, and Sundararajan, 1999). However, too-big-to-fail arguments cannot be invoked repeatedly. If the initial restructuring measures do not make a bank viable, more drastic measures to resolve failed banks should be taken. These measures could involve splitting up the bank, partially liquidating it, or engineering a major shrinkage

---

[13]See, for example, the Board of Governors of the Federal Reserve (1999) and Lang and Robertson (2000).

[14]The legal system of some countries allows losses to be imposed on subordinate debt holders without permanently closing and liquidating the banks by passing the failed bank quickly through receivership.

[15]The Gramm-Reach-Bliley Act requires large U.S. banks to issue long-term, unsecured debt if these banks control a financial subsidiary.

[16]What constitutes a bank that is "too big to fail" cannot be established universally but needs to reflect the specific features of each banking system (e.g., the size of interbank and other large credit exposures, the number of viable surviving banks able to provide needed services, etc.) and the economy.

[17]For example, systems of private deposit insurance in five U.S. states defaulted in the late 1980s and early 1990s and caused major distress to depositors in these regions when one of the two largest members of the deposit insurance system failed (English, 1993).

of its balance sheet through structural and/or operational downsizing.

Country Specifics

Many standard features should be present in a deposit insurance system, but also many country-specific conditions must be taken into account. Deposit insurance is best suited for an economy with a relatively large number of banks operating according to the same rules. However, these conditions are often not present and the most difficult cases in which to consider a deposit protection are banking systems that have a very skewed structure in terms of: (1) size—that is, one or a few very large banks and some or many small ones; (2) ownership—that is, a few dominant state-owned banks that may carry explicit or implicit guarantees of all their deposits; and, more important (3) soundness—that is, a few well-managed and solvent banks together with a significant number and share of insolvent and/or nonviable banks. As mentioned above, under (1) and (2) a deposit insurance system would require very careful design, while under (3), as further discussed in Section III, insurance would best be postponed until after the weak banks have been restructured.

Concentration

Any system of insurance seeks to diversify its risks across a number of participants in order to overcome regional or industry-specific shocks and to share the costs of failures. In many countries, however, the banking system is highly concentrated and in others concentration will follow restructuring in the aftermath of a crisis. Consequently, in these countries, it will not be possible to diversify risks across a large number of member institutions. As a result, the question must be posed whether any system of privately funded deposit insurance can work in a country with a concentrated banking system. The failure of a very large member could overwhelm a privately funded system. Private funding promotes good incentives, but leaves the system vulnerable to the collapse of a large member, raising the question: is a deposit insurance system feasible in a highly concentrated banking system?

This report suggests that a privately funded system can work and can result in a number of advantages, which may (or may not) be judged sufficient to outweigh a problem of moderate to high concentration. Insurance premiums might need to be higher than those in a country with a more diversified banking system, but this problem may be outweighed by the system's three advantages—namely, the establishment of a structure for resolution of problem banks and for distributing losses in case of bank fail-

ures, the creation of a framework for sharing the costs of individual bank failures, and the building up of an insurance fund to help pay for any losses. The deposit insurance system may replace an existing blanket guarantee of all depositors and creditors with limited coverage for small depositors. This limitation seeks to overcome the problem of excessive coverage and resulting moral hazard. More fundamentally, deposit insurance can make the banking markets contestable, if not perfectly competitive, by allowing for the possibility of new entrants into the industry.[18]

Ownership: State-Owned Banks

Governments commonly institute a system of deposit insurance when there are a few, large state-owned banks that have implicit guarantees and a number of smaller or newly-chartered private banks. The government may be in the process of privatizing the industry, may be concerned about the condition of borrowers, and may want to help the new institutions prosper, even though it buttresses competing banks with an implicit or explicit comprehensive guarantee. As discussed further in Section IV, the state banks' full guarantee will be removed in time. However, including both private and guaranteed state institutions in the insurance system helps to build the system's resources and somewhat redress the state institutions' competitive advantage. The process may work, as long as the banking system remains sound for long enough to allow the government to phase out the full guarantee. If a crisis hits soon, however, the public is likely to favor the fully guaranteed banks over the smaller private institutions and runs on the latter may ensue.

Fragility

A limited, explicit system of deposit insurance should be installed when the banking system is sound. As discussed further in Section IV, that means bank restructuring needs to have been successfully accomplished before the system is implemented. The system can be planned, the legislation prepared, and the industry and public informed of its pending arrival during the restructuring process so that it is an integral part of the measures being taken. But it should not go into operation until all interested parties agree that the financial system is strong enough to withstand the financial and administrative

---

[18]Although there may not be a large number of competitors in a contestable system, it can experience the advantages of competition. The fact that new banks can join the industry makes existing banks act competitively.

demands that deposit insurance will place upon it and until rules ensure that losses will be equitably and efficiently distributed.

Countries are often impatient and reluctant to wait for this opportune time, however. But starting a system of deposit insurance will not relieve them of their responsibility to cleanse the banking system first. Deposit protection can postpone a banking debacle, but it is unlikely to prevent one. Moreover, delaying resolution can exacerbate weak banks' problems by allowing them to gamble for recovery and lose, and, in so doing, magnify the costs of failure resolution and the possibility of contagion.

But a country may have more legitimate reasons for starting a system of deposit insurance. It may want to increase savings, encourage the development of the banking system, and modernize the payment system. In this case, it may announce that an insurance system will commence in one to two years with membership that will be restricted to sound, eligible institutions. In the interim, the supervisor, in consultation with the incipient system, will determine which institutions are sound enough to qualify. The supervisor should notify those institutions not considered sufficiently sound and give them one year to meet the desired standards. Those that do not qualify would be excluded from the system, which would probably lead to their demise.

If the government were to authorize a system of deposit insurance while banks that are too weak to join are still operating, it risks runs, possibly systemic runs. Where the number and size of the weak nonmembers is small, danger to the system may not be great but the government must be prepared to take over and resolve those banks that the public judges to be nonviable. If the number and/or the size of the weak banks is large, the government should wait to install a system until the banking system is stronger.

Avoiding Moral Hazard

As mentioned earlier, deposit insurance can create incentive incompatibilities that weaken the banking system and make the cost of insurance prohibitive. Thus, a deposit protection system needs to be designed to provide a set of inducements (that include both positive and negative reinforcements—"carrots and sticks") to encourage all of the parties involved (small depositors, large depositors, and other creditors, owners, boards of directors, managers, borrowers, supervisors, judges, government officials, and legislators) to act in ways that serve to strengthen the banking system (Kane, 1992).

To avoid the pitfalls of poor incentives and high cost, a system of deposit insurance should include

several standard features, which are summarized in Table 1. For example, to minimize moral hazard, the system should be explicitly and clearly established in the law so that all bank customers know the rules under which the system operates. As discussed earlier, those rules include the supervisors having a system of prompt remedial actions to remedy bank problems and power to close or otherwise resolve failed depository institutions promptly when remedial action is not successful. In addition, deposit coverage should be low.

This section discusses steps that can be taken to contain moral hazard, including obtaining and publishing information on the condition of individual banks, choosing which financial instruments to cover, and which to exclude, setting the level of coverage, considering adopting coinsurance, netting outstanding loans against deposits, and determining who shall have priority over the assets of the intervened bank.

Make the Deposit Insurance System Transparent

Transparency is essential because it allows bank customers to protect their interests. Transparency requires explicitly defining the deposit guarantee in law and/or regulation, clarifying what qualifies as an insured deposit, allowing the supervisor to have information on individual banks (which allows swift remedial actions), and disseminating nonproprietary information to the public.

Explicitly Define the System in Law and/or Regulation

Explicitly formulated systems have advantages over implicit schemes. For example, the rules of the system (particularly those relating to limited coverage) that are known to the public and adhered to by the authorities promote good governance by owners and managers and encourage discipline by sophisticated creditors. Making the laws and regulations transparent and disclosing bank-specific information allows the public to protect its interests by requiring interest rate premiums from banks that have risky portfolios and judiciously entrusting their funds to the soundest banks. Such restraint on risk taking reduces the government's exposure to loss when banks default because it warns a bank's large customers that taking excessive risks can be costly to them.

Define Deposits

It is the juxtaposition of the characteristics of a bank's assets (which are typically longer-term, illiquid, and difficult-to-value loans) and its liabilities (which are mainly deposits) that make banks vulnerable to runs. While different countries include different instruments in their classification of "deposit," the essence of the debt instrument is that it is repayable at par, often on demand.

One of the most crucial pieces of information that the public needs is a clear and enforceable definition of what is a deposit. The definition of a deposit—its principal and interest—will need to be clearly defined in law; regulations can provide specific details. Precision and legal enforceability are important in order to provide certainty regarding coverage and to facilitate the resolution of disputes. The definition of "deposits" should be consistent with those adopted under other banking laws and regulations. Thus, the definition chosen may vary from country to country.[19] Clear definitions will avoid much of the uncertainty and potential litigation that could otherwise occur after an institution is closed. Such definitions will also be needed to enable the deposit insurance agency to calculate the premiums (or ex post assessments) that member institutions must pay.

Both the deposit insurance agency and the institutions covered by that agency carry a responsibility to publicize which deposits are insured and which are not. The public has a right to know this, in order to protect its interests. Coverage needs to be specified in advance, and not be subject to interpretation after a failure has occurred. In each deposit or borrowing document, the issuing institutions would have to indicate in conspicuous print (to be stipulated in guidelines) whether it is insured by the deposit insurer or not. Requiring other nonbank financial institutions to disclose in each deposit/borrowing document that their instruments are not covered by deposit insurance would also need to be considered.

Information for the Supervisor and the Deposit Insurance Agency

To institute prompt remedial actions and effect speedy intervention when necessary, the supervisor needs accurate and timely information on the condition of each bank. That information is derived primarily from reports submitted by banks and from onsite inspections. But supervisors may also look to the markets for indications of bank condition. Having to pay premium interest rates on both retail and wholesale (including interbank) deposits or other liabilities including subordinated debt, or losing their ability to obtain funds, suggest that the supervisors should closely monitor the bank.

The deposit insurance authority with a broad mandate needs to know the condition of the banking industry in general and of weak institutions that might impose costs upon it so that it may plan for payouts and choose resolution strategies. Further, it needs data on the national distribution of deposits by size, so that it can choose where to set coverage limits, and the distribution in individual weak banks, so that it can forecast the financial demands that might be placed upon it. The narrowly focused agency needs data on the deposits that it guarantees.

Finding a way for the supervisor in a deposit insurance agency to share information and satisfy each agency's specific information needs is a challenge. Sharing is preferable, in the main, to duplicating oversight responsibilities, but country practices in this regard differ indeed. Good practices for sharing information with domestic or foreign supervisors are still being developed. However, the law should specify what information the deposit insurer is entitled to receive and what information the supervisor is obliged to convey promptly. Where the deposit insurance authority has a narrow range of responsibilities, the flow of information on the condition of the banking industry in general, on individual institutions, and, particularly, on vulnerable institutions, and on deposit levels will be one way—from the supervisor to the deposit insurance agency. However, where the deposit insurer has a broader role and independent sources of data, the law should require that the agency should reciprocally share its own information with the supervisor. The law should also require that agency staff obey the same rules as supervisors regarding the confidentiality of information.

Disseminating Information

Supervisors will want to disseminate as much of their information as is competitively equitable to enable the public to protect its financial interests and to help keep the banking system sound through market discipline. Accurate information will also help to avoid unnecessary runs against sound banks. The supervisor must also make arrangements to share a larger portion of its bank-by-bank data with the deposit insurance agency so that it is not blindsided by the unexpected failure of one of its member institutions. Sharing information is more problematic where the deposit insurance system is privately run. In this situation, questions of confidentiality and competitive fairness arise.

Coverage

Issues related to coverage include deciding which classes of depository institution should be required to join the system of deposit insurance, which financial

---

[19]The defining characteristic of a deposit is that it has a fixed principal. See Garcia (1996) for a discussion of the characteristics of a deposit and why offering deposits makes banks vulnerable to insolvency and illiquidity.

instruments to cover, and to what extent to cover them.

Which Institutions to Cover?

Clearly those institutions that offer deposits are the prime candidates for coverage by the system of deposit insurance. Including a wide range of institutions in the system in order to diversify its risks has advantages, but these advantages are not always compelling. Where some institutions are not subject to the same stringent prudential regulations as commercial banks, they may be excluded from the system. A country may choose to institute a separate scheme to cover such depository institutions. This scheme may offer lower coverage, or charge higher premiums in order to cover the additional risks attendant on inferior prudential oversight.

Which Instruments to Cover?

This section discusses which instruments to cover by deposit insurance and the limits on, and exclusions from, coverage. It is administratively simpler to protect deposits of all types rather than to confine coverage to natural persons or to exclude certain deposits. Administrative simplicity can accelerate compensation, and promptness in payment is critical to the credibility of a deposit insurer. (This principle is often overlooked, as the survey in Section III shows that payment is typically slow.) Excluding classes of deposits and depositors delays payment. The following bullet points list the types of deposits to be included, and establish that both principal and interest would be covered.

- Deposits of all types, including demand, savings, and time deposits that are denominated in domestic currency, should be covered.
- Promissory notes that are often issued by finance companies would be covered by the system if finance companies are allowed to join the scheme, and if they are defined by law and/or regulated by the deposit insurance agency as deposits.
- Both principal and any accrued interest that has not already been added to the principal would be covered. Interest coverage could be determined on the basis of what has been booked at the date of intervention, even if it has not yet been added to the principal. Where it is general practice to credit interest frequently to a depositor's account, not covering interest would be more time consuming and costly to administer than covering it. However, depositors in troubled institutions typically receive higher interest rates. The deposit insurance authority should have no obligation to pay such high rates after taking charge of an institution. Consideration might be given to imposing a cap (for example, the average rate paid by the five largest banks for any maturity) on the rates paid on deposits in failed banks.
- The coverage to be provided for the deposit of trusts, managed, and provident funds would have to be defined. For trust accounts, one person should be designated to represent the group, which would be entitled only to coverage for a single person.

Foreign currency deposits. The decision whether to cover deposits denominated in foreign currencies is more complex. The choice will depend on the country's particular circumstances. Where most transactions are conducted in the domestic currency and the total value of retail foreign currency deposits is small, the authorities may choose not to extend coverage to deposits of foreign currency, without risking runs. But where foreign currency deposits are widely used, and particularly where the country is dollarized, the deposit insurance system may insure foreign currency deposits to promote financial stability.

Guaranteeing that deposits will be repaid in foreign currencies exposes the deposit insurer to risks that are not easily managed. Consequently, a number of countries compensate individual holders of foreign currency deposits in domestic currency. This is the appropriate choice. The law or regulation governing coverage must spell out that the conversion from foreign to domestic currency will be made at the exchange rate that prevails at some uniform and clearly specified time. Yet, even providing to pay foreign currency deposits in domestic currency will not protect the system from the loss it will incur if the domestic currency depreciates after the deposit is made.

Which Instruments to Exclude?

Although there are advantages to covering deposits of all types up to a low coverage limit, experience has shown that countries exclude a number of categories of deposits from coverage for a variety of reasons. The European Union Directive on Deposit Guarantee Schemes permits these exclusions and a number of countries have adopted them. A list of items that can be excluded from coverage under the deposit insurance directive appears in Box 1. The survey in Section III details country practices regarding exclusions.

- The exclusion of bearer instruments can be justified because it would be impossible to implement the required limitations on coverage.

Other Nonessential Exclusions

It is not essential to exclude insider deposits (e.g., those pertaining to owners, managers, and their fami-

---

Box 1. Exclusions from Deposit Insurance Coverage

Article 7(2) of the European Union's Directive on Deposit Insurance permits member countries to exclude certain categories of deposits from coverage. The exclusions are *not* mandatory. The exclusions (laid out in Annex I to the Directive) are listed below.

Official Journal of the
No. L 135/12   European Communities   31.5.94

ANNEX I
List of exclusions referred to in Article 7(2)

1. Deposits by financial institutions as defined in Article 1(6) of Directive 89/646/EEC.
2. Deposits by insurance undertakings.
3. Deposits by government and central administrative authorities.
4. Deposits by provincial, regional, local and municipal authorities.
5. Deposits by collective investment undertakings.
6. Deposits by pension and retirement funds.
7. Deposits by a credit institution's own directors, managers, members personally liable, holders of at least 5% of the credit institution's capital, persons responsible for carrying out the statutory audits of the credit institution's accounting documents and depositors of similar status in other companies in the same group.
8. Deposits by close relatives and third parties acting on behalf of the depositors referred to in 7.
9. Deposits by other companies in the same group.
10. Non-nominative deposits.
11. Deposits for which the depositor has, on an individual basis, obtained from the same credit institution rates and financial concessions which have helped to aggravate its financial situation.
12. Debt securities issued by the same institution and liabilities arising out of own acceptances and promissory notes.
13. Deposits in currencies other than:
    • those of the Member States;
    • ECU's.
14. Deposits by companies which are of such a size that they are not permitted to draw up abridged balance sheets pursuant to Article 11 of the Fourth Council Directive (78/660/EEC) of 25 July 1978 based on Article 53(3)(g) of the Treaty on the annual accounts of certain types of companies.[1]

---

[1]OJ No. L 222, 14.8.1978, p. 11. Directive as last amended by Directive 90/605/EEC (OJ No. L 317, 16.11.1990, p. 60).

---

supervision and dealt with by the legal system should supervisory prevention fail. Some countries exclude deposits carrying excessively high interest rates from coverage. Paying high rates can indicate that the institution is weak, is bidding up rates to retain funds, or is trying to grow and gamble for recovery. Such actions can harm social competitors when they raise the general level of rates paid on deposits. However, the supervisor should deal with such problems rather than encumber the deposit insurance system with a supervisory responsibility. Similarly, the judiciary should deal with problems relating to money laundering and other illegal activities. The deposit insurance agency cannot address these problems by excluding illegal deposits from coverage. Many countries in the survey excluded interbank deposits, but if coverage is low, including them in the guarantee will not encourage moral hazard.

Extent of Coverage

To fulfill its basic mandate of protecting consumers, the deposit insurance scheme should be designed to protect small depositors who are likely to have low incomes, be unsophisticated in the ways of banks and lending, and lack the time, information, and means to study the condition of their bank. Excluding larger depositors and unsecured creditors from coverage, thereby exposing them to loss, will cause these depositors to monitor the condition of their banks carefully and to impose market pressure on the banks to remain sound. This discipline will support the supervisors' efforts to encourage institutions to remain strong. The presence of deposit insurance also removes two of the obstacles to taking stern measures to resolve nonviable institutions—the fear of imposing losses on small depositors, and the political repercussions of doing so. In turn, the fear of closure will encourage remaining banks to maintain high standards.

Coverage for Each Deposit or Each Depositor?

Compensation should be paid up to the limit on the sum of deposits held by one individual depositor in any member institution. Holders of joint accounts would elect one of the group as the primary depositor, and coverage would apply to him/her in conformity with national law. Currently only a few countries deviate from this arrangement. Some (the United States and Canada) offer more generous coverage on joint and retirement accounts. Others offered coverage on each and every deposit in an institution, but no longer do so. It would be possible to impose a limit on the number of times that claims for insurance can be filed in any year or over a lifetime, but there has been limited interest in doing so.

---

lies). Insiders often receive special privileges, such as priority in bank lending, and such loans can weaken a bank, but these problems can be prevented by careful

The problem with coverage per deposit is that it would allow a depositor to easily guarantee a large amount of funds in different accounts within a single institution. The European Union has moved away from coverage per deposit and toward coverage per depositor since the EU Directive on Deposit Guarantee Schemes was issued in 1994. It remains possible for a depositor under coverage-per-depositor to obtain multiple coverage by diversifying his/her funds across accounts in different institutions, which is an attractive way for depositors to limit their exposure. Nevertheless, coverage-per-depositor does not extend coverage to large aggregate holdings in individual banks.

Amount of Coverage

The aggregate amount of coverage offered to each depositor in any bank should be relatively low. As a starting point, coverage could be considered in the region of one or two times per capita GDP, but the limit may be set with more precision by examining the distribution of deposits by size. Within this distribution, the limit should be set to cover the majority of the total number of deposits (say, 80 to 90 percent of the number of deposits), but only a smaller percentage of the total value of deposits (say, 20 percent of the value of all deposits).[20] Each country should conduct a careful assessment of the level of coverage that will strike a balance between discouraging destabilizing runs by small depositors while retaining market discipline from larger depositors. The country may also set its coverage level with a view to maintaining the international competitiveness of its banks.

As shown in Figure 1, the limits to the full coverage that countries provide vary widely—from more than eight times per capita GDP in Oman to less than the level of per capita GDP in some Central and Eastern European countries. If a depositor's holdings exceed the amount covered under the system, the depositor will take a place in line with other creditors to receive the proceeds recovered over time from the assets of the failed bank. Alternatively, as in a number of countries, there could be coinsurance above the basic coverage.

Coinsurance

To encourage market discipline, some countries require all depositors to bear risk on all of their de-posits. Coinsurance has the advantage of assuring depositors of the prompt repayment of at least part of their deposit. It is often run on a sliding scale, so that depositors recover, say, 90 percent of a small tranche of their deposit, a smaller percentage of the second tranche, and successively smaller percentages of the subsequent tranches. This practice is not optimal, however, because it fails to provide basic consumer protection and therefore does little to prevent small depositors from triggering a run. A more acceptable system is to cover the smallest tranche of deposits in full and impose a haircut on larger deposits.[21] Above-the-limit coinsurance will increase total coverage somewhat. This type of coinsurance may encourage savings, but has two disadvantages. First, it is more difficult for the public to understand and, second, it may increase the cost of resolving failed banks. Consequently, a country may want to carefully consider the relative costs and benefits of installing more than two tranches. The advantage that coinsurance provides—quick access to larger depositors' funds—can also be obtained if a deposit insurer with a broad mandate provides uninsured depositors with an advance payment to uninsured depositors of part of what the system estimates it will recover from the failed banks' assets.

Should the Coverage Limit Be Indexed to Inflation?

Although some countries index the coverage limit for inflation, good practice argues against indexing, as this leads to annual changes that would be difficult for depositors to remember. Being able to keep track of the coverage limit is essential for enabling the public to protect its interests. The ideal situation is one where a country has low inflation, so that it can keep the limit constant for a relatively long period of time until the increasing value of real GDP warrants an increase. In this way, the public can know the coverage limit with certainty and the limit remains appropriate to the number and value of deposits in the economy. When adjustments are necessary, however, it may be better to delay changing the coverage limit, until an easy-to-remember number becomes appropriate.

Netting Deposits Against Loans

It is sometimes suggested that the receiver or liquidator of a failed bank, rather than paying a depositor directly in full, should offset (i.e., net or set off) deposits against any obligations the depositor has to

---

[20]Country practices in this regard are detailed in Table A5 of the Statistical Appendix. The table reveals that it is indeed feasible to compensate a high percentage of the number of depositors and a low percentage of the value of deposits, because most deposits are small.

[21]Some countries impose haircuts on a sliding scale, but this can violate the principle that simplicity, transparency, and public trust go hand-in-hand.

Figure 1. Ratios of Deposit Coverage to per capita GDP in Selected Countries, 2000

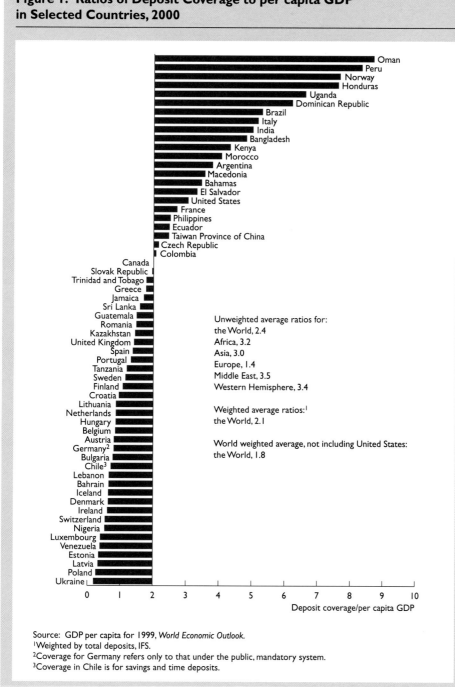

Unweighted average ratios for:
the World, 2.4
Africa, 3.2
Asia, 3.0
Europe, 1.4
Middle East, 3.5
Western Hemisphere, 3.4

Weighted average ratios:[1]
the World, 2.1

World weighted average, not including United States:
the World, 1.8

Deposit coverage/per capita GDP

Source: GDP per capita for 1999, *World Economic Outlook.*
[1]Weighted by total deposits, IFS.
[2]Coverage for Germany refers only to that under the public, mandatory system.
[3]Coverage in Chile is for savings and time deposits.

the bank (see Box 2).[22] Offsetting loans that are in default is appropriate, but offsetting loans that are

current could destroy a healthy business that may, for example, be unable to find a quick replacement for its working capital. Thus, the approach that is recommended below has been adopted in a number of countries in order to find a balance between two considerations.

[22]A cross-default clause, often used by payment clearing houses and interbank contracts, automatically invokes netting under specified conditions.

Box 2. Offsetting Loans Against Deposits

Two fundamental questions arise regarding offsetting.

One question asks whether netting should apply regardless of the status of the loan or whether it should occur only when the loan is due or in default. Netting against performing loans could prejudice the viability of sound businesses whose loans, in effect, are called and are thus simultaneously deprived of their liquid assets. Consequently, netting is almost universally confined to cases where the loan has matured or is in default.[1]

Another question relates to the status of the deposit. When legal bankruptcy occurs, all claims become due and payable immediately. However, a liquidator or receiver might not want to pay out the full amount of the principal and accrued interest on a long-term deposit that carries a below market rate. He would prefer to offer the lower, net present value of the deposit, which would conserve deposit insurance resources. But he can do so only if there is a special provision in the law permitting him to do so.

There are *opposing views* on netting and country practices diverge in applying the concept.

One view, typically taken in countries in the Anglo-American tradition, stresses that it is important to protect the creditors of the failed bank by maximizing the amount recovered from its assets and so favors offsetting matured mutual claims. They argue that it is unjust that a defaulting borrower should insist on payment of his deposit but not service his loan, that netting protects creditors and reduces the transmission of failure from one bank to another, reduces litigation and, thus, the cost of credit, and prevents the bank's borrower from being bankrupted unnecessarily when he has funds already available. (Countries favoring this view are listed in the first column of Table 4 of Garcia, 1996.)

The other view, espoused in Franco-Latin countries, considers that offsetting departs from the principle of equal treatment of creditors. In general, the authorities in these countries also consider that netting is inequitable to debtors and so they prohibit it when insolvency occurs because the creditor gets paid in full (up to the amount of the deposit), but the depositor may receive only a portion of his funds. (For countries opposing this view, see the second column of Table 4 in Garcia, 1996).

However, there is also an issue concerning *netting in relation to deposit insurance*. It should be noted that offsetting also gives borrowers a priority over the assets of the failed bank as compared to other depositors because it grants, in effect, a speedy and 100 percent coverage of the deposit that is offset against a loan. Other depositors have to stand in line to obtain the more limited coverage available under the deposit insurance system or from the proceeds obtained when the bank is liquidated. It would, for example, be possible for a depositor who is concerned about the condition of his bank to take out a loan immediately before the bank is closed and so obtain full and speedy coverage for his deposit. However, a more telling argument is that, by offsetting unpaid obligations against insured deposits, the liquidator or receiver can reduce the cost of the payoff to the deposit insurance system.

Finally, netting becomes more complex *where the deposit insurer and the liquidator/receiver* of the failed bank are separate entities than where there is no deposit insurance system or the system is also the receiver (as in the United States). With separate agencies, the deposit insurance system compensates insured depositors, and seeks recompense from the liquidator/receiver who takes ownership of the bank's assets and uses the proceeds from their liquidation to repay the deposit insurer, uninsured depositors, and other creditors.[2] Then, special agreements have to be formalized to make netting feasible.

---

[1]See, for example, Sections 53–55 of the Bankruptcy Code of the Netherlands. However, some countries (e.g., Peru) net all types of deposits against loans regardless of status.

[2]Each country's law will determine the priority of claims among these groups. Such priorities are discussed further in Garcia (1996, pp. 39–41 and Appendix I).

The first consideration is providing incentives for borrowers to service their loans now and in the future, and for depositors and other bank creditors to continue to trust the banking system. The second consideration is minimizing costs to the deposit insurer.

When a depositor is also a debtor of the failed bank, his/her deposit should be netted (offset) against the loan, but only if it is overdue or delinquent. It would be unfair to other depositors if the holder of a delinquent loan, especially one that has contributed to the failure of the bank, were to benefit from insurance coverage. Hence, the balance of the defaulter's deposit should be netted (offset) against his overdue loan(s). Loans that are current, however, should not be offset against a borrower's deposits. To do so could unfairly deprive a good borrower of working capital and prejudice his ability to continue in business. Accordingly, this paper recommends that the insured parts of deposits of all kinds be netted against:

- claims that have already fallen due or are delinquent;
- promised, but undelivered, subscriptions from shareholders; and

- damage assessments against owners and managers.[23]

Offsetting would also be restricted to situations where both the bank's and the customer's claims are well-documented, can be settled easily, are not subject to dispute, and were established well before the bank became insolvent.[24] If the value of the loan exceeds that of the deposits, the remainder of the loan would continue to exist as a claim against the debtor.

These recommended principles would need to be firmly established in the insolvency law of the country, perhaps as an administrative-law exception to the general bankruptcy law that would govern bank failures and depositor protection. For example, the governing law or contract would lay down the basic process for determining who gets what, and in what order. It is recognized that it may prove difficult to graft these principles on to some legal frameworks.

Reducing Adverse Selection

There are two design features for the system of deposit insurance that will help to reduce the incidence of adverse selection, which occurs when the weakest institutions choose to join a voluntary system, while the strongest remain outside. Such a system is unlikely to remain financially viable. First, membership should be compulsory. In particular, the system should not allow members to leave the system when they choose to do so, and they certainly should not receive a refund of their accumulated contributions. Second, when a deposit insurer has gained experience, it may institute a system of risk-adjusted premiums to reward stronger banks within the compulsory system.

Make Membership Compulsory

Membership in the system should be mandatory for all institutions located in the country, including specialized state-owned banks that accept deposits and are supervised by the supervisory authority. Otherwise, only the weakest institutions will join and the system will not be financially viable. Membership should be broad because the cost of the insurance must be shared among a wide number of institutions, if the scheme is to remain financially viable. Although compulsory membership involves a degree of cross-subsidization by strong institutions of weak ones, *all* members, even the strongest ones, benefit from having a more stable industry with reduced fear of depositor runs. The stronger institutions should be required to pay for that privilege.

Include State-Owned Institutions

The playing field needs to be level for all deposit-taking institutions to encourage competition. Thus, government-owned institutions that take deposits should also be required to join the deposit insurance system and pay premiums at the same rate as other members, even if they are initially the beneficiaries of an implicit full government guarantee that the government plans to phase out later. Government-owned institutions should also be supervised to the same standards as other insurance participants and ultimately receive the same coverage as private institutions. Thus, a country's banking act might need to be revised to bring the regulation and supervision of state-owned institutions under the supervisory authority. Finally, at an opportune moment, as discussed further in Section III, the full implicit or explicit guarantee for state-owned institutions should be removed.

Institutional Membership: Inclusions and Exclusions

Membership should be compulsory for all eligible members. These would include:

- All domestic banks and other deposit-taking institutions explicitly encompassed by the system of deposit insurance according to the law.
- All branches and subsidiaries of foreign banks operating onshore. Foreign institutions should regard paying insurance premiums as a cost of doing business in a country. Sometimes the deposits of a foreign bank are covered under banks' domestic insurance system. The host country can supplement the coverage offered abroad where that coverage is for a smaller amount and it can accept foreign coverage if the amount insured is larger. Doing the latter, however, may give foreign banks an advantage in the domestic market.[25]
- Finance companies, credit unions, and cooperatives would join the system as long as they faced the same prudential regulations and were supervised by the same agency as banks and other insured depository institutions. Allowing

---

[23]As, for example, in Sections 53–55 of the Bankruptcy Code of the Netherlands and the FDIC's Manual on Band Liquidation in the United States.

[24]It would be counterproductive to protect a depositor with inside information who has taken out a loan just before the bank fails.

---

[25]The EU Directive sets rules governing coverage from other EU countries.

institutions that are not strictly supervised to join would not be fair to those members that face stringent regulations, as the more loosely supervised firms are more likely to impose losses on the fund. The government, however, may consider establishing separate deposit insurance schemes for credit unions and cooperatives (possibly with lower coverage limits).

Some countries consider that the purpose of the deposit insurance scheme is to protect the deposits of residents; consequently, they exclude nonresidents. Systems in other countries cover nonresidents, however, to encourage deposits from nonresidents.

When considering the treatment of nonresidents and foreign institutions, the following good practice applies:

- Banks operating offshore would be excluded. The exclusion would cover foreign branches and subsidiaries and units of domestic banks that operate offshore. The objective of the insurance scheme is to protect domestic residents from loss, not foreign residents. In nondollarized economies, this aim would be achieved by covering only domestic currency deposits.

Risk-Adjusting Premiums

A system of risk-based premiums is logically satisfying, but it is not easy to administer. Nevertheless, as the survey in Section III shows, more than one-third of countries with explicit deposit insurance schemes is currently using systems of risk-based premiums.[26] This is a recent development and contrasts with the findings of Kyei (1995).

The objective of risk-adjusting premiums is to require riskier institutions that are more likely to call upon assistance from the deposit insurer to pay more for coverage. Yet insurance always contains an element of cross-subsidization of the weakest members by the strongest. The principles of actuarial accuracy and cross-subsidization are both desirable up to a point, but they conflict. Thus, a balance has to be struck, as in all insurance contracts, between the two principles. Moreover, there is a second conflict. Setting the premiums to reflect the risk an institution poses to the fund can be complex. Yet, there are advantages to having a system that is easy for the consumer and the markets to understand. Choosing an appropriate balance between actuarial accuracy and simplicity is a challenge.

As a result, the architects of a newly created deposit insurance system are advised to "keep it simple" until they have gained experience in implementing the system. Simplicity may involve charging uniform premiums until system staff become experienced enough to tackle the complex task of adjusting deposit insurance premiums for risk.

Techniques for Risk-Adjustment

Nevertheless, countries that have had systems in place for some time are now moving toward risk-adjustment. In the process they have adopted a number of approaches to adjusting the premiums that banks pay to reflect the risk they impose on the system. One straightforward method is to ask banks to pay premiums based on their risk-adjusted assets, rather than on their deposits. This approach imposes no additional costs of calculation on banks and might be a good starting point for a country wanting to move away from premiums set uniformly on deposits in all banks. While the current system of risk-adjustment for assets under the Basel Capital Accord is crude, it is in the process of being refined.

A second approach is to charge lower premiums to banks that have higher capital ratios and/or supervisory ratings. The FDIC in the United States takes both capital and CAMELS ratings into account.[27] Other countries use more complex systems for assessing risk.[28] These ratings are typically not disclosed to the public on an individual-bank basis.

Minimizing Agency Problems

A deposit insurance scheme may be privately, publicly, or jointly funded and operated. In any of these arrangements, problems (called "agency problems") can occur when an agent serves his own interests rather than those of the principal who employs him. These principal–agent relationships can be complex in deposit insurance systems and give rise to three kinds of agency problems—political interference, regulatory capture, and interagency conflicts. In turn, this problem can result in high fiscal costs.

In the case of deposit insurance, some consideration has to be given to identifying who is the agent and who is the principal. Whether the deposit insurance agency is publicly or privately run, the agency,

---

[26]The Bank Insurance Fund in the United States introduced risk-based premiums in 1992 and subsequently increased the premium range to stretch from zero basis points for the strongest banks (judged on the basis of their capital ratios and supervisory ratings) to 27 basis points for the weakest banks. It is currently considering a new system to give greater actuarial accuracy.

[27]Under the CAMELS system, banks are rated on a scale from one to five according to a composite of the *c*apital adequacy, *a*sset quality, *m*anagement capability, *e*arnings, *l*iquidity, and *s*ensitivity to systemic risk.

[28]The basis for risk-assessment is discussed further in the survey in Section III and Table A4 of the Statistical Appendix.

acting to protect the interests of depositors, is the agent. In a privately run system, the banks are the principals because they both fund and govern the system. (The system should be funded by the member banks themselves to limit government outlays and provide peer pressure for safety.) In a privately funded scheme that has government financial backing, however, the government may or may not run the scheme. When the government runs a privately funded scheme, it, acting on behalf of taxpayers, and the banks are both principals. The deposit insurance system is still the agent that acts for the depositors.

Government backing tends to bolster a system's credibility. Hence it is no surprise that government backing is provided for all but the strongest banking systems. The overriding argument in favor of a government-run scheme is financial integrity. To limit conflicts of interest, a system with public backing is best run by a government agency. A second best solution is to have a system jointly operated by the government and the banks, but where bankers do not dominate the board of directors.[29] Allowance can be made for input from the banking industry through an advisory committee to the board.

If publicly or jointly run, the agency can be integral with, or separate from, the central bank and the supervisory agency. In either case, conflicts between the interests of the monetary authority, the banking supervisor, and the deposit insurer can occur both within departments of the same agency and across separate agencies. In addition, the deposit protection system can become captured by the industry, and interagency conflicts may occur, but these problems can occur also in a privately run scheme.

Political Interference

The first agency problem, which applies particularly to a government-run scheme, is interference by politicians in the operations of banks, in their supervision, and/or in the insurance function. This problem can be contained by sanctioning interference and by making the agency an independent organization that is nevertheless accountable to the government and/or the legislature for its actions, operations, and administration. The agency needs to be supported by a clear legal and regulatory framework to limit political interference. Prohibiting, limiting, and/or publicly disclosing financial contributions to campaign funds for elected officials, especially those with responsibilities for overseeing financial agencies, will help to contain political interference. Transparency in its operations also

helps because it allows the press to report untoward actions and the public to scrutinize the system in order to protect its position as bank customer and/or taxpayer.

Regulatory Capture

The second agency problem is regulatory capture—a situation where the deposit insurance agency serves the banks, rather than the interests of the public at large as depositors and taxpayers. In a privately run and funded scheme, bankers are appropriately in charge, so the problem arises only when a privately funded scheme has government financial backing. The danger of capture can be reduced by having the government run the scheme even though it is "owned" by the banks, by not allowing bankers to dominate the agency's board of directors, and by taking other steps to keep agency officials focused on their public responsibilities.

Bankers have useful perspectives on the banking situation and need a forum for expressing their interests regarding deposit insurance, so they may form a consultative committee to the board of directors of the deposit guarantee system. The system's managers and staff should be trained to keep their public responsibilities in mind when executing their duties. Having to report publicly to the administration and the legislature will give the public an opportunity to assess the system's performance of its public trust. Staff may be precluded from accepting honoraria or from taking positions at member institutions for a number of years after they leave the agency.

Interagency Friction

The third agency problem is a lack of cooperation between or within financial regulatory agencies. On occasion, there can be disputes leading to hostility. This situation can occur, for example, where the deposit insurer depends on the supervisor for information about institutions in the system, and on the central bank for macroeconomic insights, but where the supervisor and the monetary authority are unable or unwilling to provide necessary information.

To help remedy this problem, the objectives and functions of different financial authorities must be clarified. The functions include monetary policy, supervision, deposit insurance, bank restructuring, and fiscal policy. Such clarity of purpose is more important than the institutional location, which often is determined by the availability of scarce banking skills, human constraints, short-term legal impediments, etc. Especially in a small country with a shortage of skilled personnel, the central bank, as the monetary authority, may also be responsible for bank supervi-

---

[29]Nevertheless, as discussed later, some privately run systems are operating successfully.

sion and deposit insurance.[30] Where resources are greater, there is much to be said for keeping the responsibility for deposit insurance separate from the supervisory authority and the central bank. A ministry of finance could be involved because of its responsibility for systemic bank restructuring, but the preference is to have the deposit insurer not report to the ministry. Regardless of their institutional location, there would need to be close cooperation between these different authorities.

If separate, the deposit insurance agency needs to consult with the other agencies to assure that it has adequate information. It is uneconomical for the system to establish a duplicate structure for banking supervision. The consultation may be facilitated by including members of the other agencies on the system's board. In a public or quasi-public system, the board of directors should not be dominated by bankers, who, as mentioned earlier, have a conflict of interest and may try to transfer costs from banks to the government. In a private system of deposit insurance, the board of directors should include a representative from the bank supervisory agency.

Collaboration and Information Sharing with the Supervisor

If the deposit insurance agency is to carry out its responsibilities successfully, it must be assured of access to necessary information and cooperation from the supervisory and other government authorities.

- The paybox deposit insurance agency, whether public or private, must receive from the supervisor the names and addresses of the depositors that are to be compensated and the amounts due to them.

A broad deposit insurance agency will also need data on bank conditions. Where the agency is run by the government, communication problems can be reduced by placing a legal obligation on the supervisor and the central bank to provide the necessary information. The deposit insurer, the central bank, and the supervisory agency can also be required to cooperate closely. However, where the broad agency is purely private, the problem is more difficult to resolve. The supervisor would be appropriately reluctant to divulge data on bank conditions that would give a competitive advantage to those banks that provide board members to the agency. However, for a publicly run deposit insurance system:

- The legislation should require a smooth flow of information and close cooperation among the deposit insurance agency, the supervisor, central bank, and the ministry of finance. What information will be shared, and under what circumstances, needs to be carefully studied and agreed upon. This includes the extent to which the supervisor should be required to provide examination and other supervisory reports to the agency. To enable the quick resolution of a failed entity, the deposit insurer must receive information from the supervisor at an early stage to make necessary preparations.
- As discussed above, the broad deposit insurance agency should be able to request the supervisor to undertake a special examination of any insured financial institution that it feels may be in financial difficulties. Whether agency staff should be able to participate in onsite inspections would vary from country to country.

The deposit insurance authority would have no supervisory responsibilities beyond the right to receive information from the supervisor and request special onsite examinations. In some countries, it could be required to report to a government agency, such as the ministry of finance, in cases where it has concerns over a bank's condition, but where the supervisor fails to take action.

Relations with the Lender of Last Resort

It is the role of the lender of last resort, not the deposit insurer, to lend to solvent but illiquid banks, and to sterilize that lending where it is necessary to keep within appropriate limits for reserve money growth, to discourage runs against them by uninsured depositors. The insurer's role is to compensate depositors. The insurer with a broad mandate will also deal with insolvent, nonviable banks and resolve them in a cost-effective and incentive-compatible manner. However, there can also be a conflict of interest between the broad system of deposit insurance and the lender of last resort. The latter organization may be unduly willing (especially where its support is covered by high-quality collateral) to provide lender-of-last-resort assistance to troubled banks, which will delay closure and increase the costs for the insurance system.[31] To reduce this problem, both the deposit insurance and central bank laws may need to be written to ensure a consistent legal framework that facilitates close cooperation between the insurance system and the lender of last resort/central bank.

---

[30]The central bank's multiple role may involve it in conflicts of interest, so countries with enough resources sometimes choose to spread the roles among different agencies.

[31]The United States found that excessive lender-of-last-resort lending had been a problem in the 1980s. It responded to this problem in legislation passed in 1991 that limited the ability of the Federal Reserve to lend to insolvent banks even against first rate collateral. See the Congressional Report accompanying the passage of the FDIC Improvement Act of 1991.

The problem of excessive lender-of-last-resort lending arises partly because it is difficult to distinguish between illiquidity and insolvency. Because a lender of last resort that lends to insolvent banks causes moral hazard, raises insurance costs, and reduces monetary control, lender-of-last-resort accommodation should be fully collateralized by sound assets that would be acceptable in the private markets in normal times. But, as argued earlier, even collateralized lender-of-last-resort lending to insolvent banks should be discouraged because it prolongs the life of such banks and crowds out other creditors. However, exceptions may be made to the application of this principle in certain circumstances. For example, a central bank might provide "bridging liquidity assistance" for a short period to a bank that has just been found to be insolvent, while a resolution is sought for it. As a precaution against moral hazard, control of the bank might be taken from its owners while it awaits recapitalization, sale, or closure.

Promoting Credibility

The design of the deposit insurance agency can importantly influence its credibility.[32] Apart from the agency's role, which was discussed previously, the agency should be designed to be independent but accountable and have adequate management and staffing.

Design and Organization of a Deposit Insurance Agency

A government-financed system needs to be run by an agency with adequate authority and political independence. At the same time, the agency must be accountable for its actions, so that it does not act in an arbitrary and capricious manner. The recommendations in this section seek to provide the requisite authority, independence, and accountability.

Authority

A "paybox" may be privately run, but to ensure sufficient authority the agency with a broad mandate needs to be a government agency established by law.[33] For example, to maintain public confidence, the broad deposit insurance system must have gov-

ernment backing. In addition, the supervisor or agency will have a strong powers to deal in a strict manner with nonviable banks, terminate the interests of shareholders, and impose "haircuts" on uninsured depositors and unsecured creditors. Power to do so should be granted by law, and such responsibilities can only be exercised by a government agency. To fulfill its responsibilities, the agency will need adequate financial resources as discussed later in this section, as well as access to information as discussed earlier.

Independence

Independence is typically not a problem in a privately run deposit insurance agency, but a number of steps need to be taken to ensure independence for a government-run agency. In this context, independence refers to status within the government and to freedom from political pressure and domination by the banking industry. In a large country that has a pool of workers with sufficient financial skills, the deposit insurance agency should be separated from the central bank and the supervisory authority, since the monetary authority, the supervisor, and the agency have different, although complementary, responsibilities. In smaller countries, the central bank may have separate departments to cover monetary policy, bank supervision, and deposit insurance. Allowing these institutions to pursue separate, sometimes conflicting, objectives, while still cooperating, is a challenge.

The following best practices apply:
- Ideally, the deposit insurance authority should be separate from the supervisory and monetary authority. The supervisor and the agency have different, although complementary, responsibilities. There could be a number of conflicts of interests in normal times if all responsibilities resided with the central bank. Nevertheless, these three institutions need to cooperate, especially in times of financial stress.
- The agency should be independent of political influence. At times, the agency may need to take actions that are unpopular with certain domestic or foreign interest groups. To act according to the law in a fair and evenhanded way, agency staff must, therefore, be free from political pressure that can cause certain individuals, companies, or economic sectors to win exceptions from laws and regulations—otherwise known as "forbearance." Independence has particular consequences for the composition of the board of directors.
- The board of directors of a government-run deposit guarantee system should reflect its independent status. It should consist of either five or

---

[32]Financial sufficiency is also important and is discussed in the following section.

[33]Some countries, such as Argentina, Germany, and Peru, have successful, privately run deposit insurance systems. Privately run systems typically have a narrow mandate. Access to financial support from the government can be especially denied in order to avoid public/private conflicts of interest.

seven members, appointed for staggered terms of, say, four years. The board's size should not be unwieldy and should not be so large as to allow individual members to hide among a multitude of members. An odd number of members is needed to make securing a majority easier. Members will have security of tenure for their limited term in office, to facilitate their independence from political interference. Board members should be relieved of their positions only for gross misconduct defined in the law (using comparable standards in other of the country's laws) to avoid dismissing them for political or petty reasons. Terms in office should be staggered to provide continuity in membership and to allow experience gained not to be lost all at once.

- The board members of a government-run deposit insurance agency should be nominated by the government (the administration) and confirmed by the legislature where there is a "separation of powers;" otherwise the board members should be confirmed by the cabinet. In this way, the government would be responsible for the integrity and effectiveness of the board, and the avenue for the agency's accountability through the government to the public would be established.
- When it backs the deposit insurance fund, the government should be able to appoint board members who would have a fiduciary interest in protecting the public. Such members would serve the public interest and not focus on the particular concerns of the banking industry, sectoral interests, or politicians' preferences.
- The board of a government-run deposit insurance system should have two ex-officio members. One would represent the supervisor (the agency head or his designated representative), and one the ministry of finance (the minister or his designated representative). The government needs to be represented on the board, but should not dominate it by having a *majority* of the membership or the position of chairman. As the government will guarantee the system and bear the costs of any failures, the ministry of finance must be represented on the authority's board. The monetary authority might, but does not have to be, represented on the board.
- The remainder of the board, constituting the majority, should be drawn from outside the government. This provision serves to protect the political independence of the deposit insurance authority, and also to draw on the necessary expertise. One of these outside members should be appointed chairman.
- There should be no board members who are currently employed by financial institutions that are members of the deposit insurance system on a government-run deposit insurance agency.[34] Likewise, major shareholders of insured institutions, and other individuals with close family or financial linkages (to be defined in the banking law) with them, should not be board members. For example, the agency will have access to information about the condition of individual member institutions. It would be inappropriate to give this information to a board member who is an employee, major shareholder, or closely linked with another insured institution. This provision prevents institutions "connected" with a board member from receiving information that would give them an advantage over competitors. Moreover, bankers might suffer from a conflict of interest and try to underfund the authority, so that the government would be forced to cover additional costs. However, bankers' experience and perspectives will be valuable to the deposit insurance agency. Consequently, a consultative council of bankers should be formed to advise the authority and bring members' concerns to the attention of the board.
- Other qualifications could be specified in the deposit insurance law. For example, the law might specify that board members and senior officials should be "fit and proper," have relevant education and/or experience, and other characteristics deemed desirable.
- The law also should grant board members immunities and protection against lawsuits for official acts taken in the course of their duties.

In small countries with limited financial expertise, however, the public deposit insurer may be a separate department of the central bank, which may also contain the supervisory agency. The central bank may have difficulty in separating its responsibilities as guardian of monetary policy and lender of last resort from those of supervising banks and running the system of deposit insurance, even if lodged in a separate department. Moreover, the objectives of the three entities may conflict. For example, by relying on its priority as a collateralized lender over the assets of the failed bank, the last resort lender may be too ready to provide liquidity assistance to a troubled bank because it is sure of getting its money back. But in being overly willing to provide liquidity assistance to prevent the bank from failing, it frequently imposes additional losses on the deposit insurer and uninsured

---

[34]Nevertheless, a number of countries have successful privately run deposit insurance systems that do have bankers on the board. Obtaining confidential information remains a problem to be overcome for privately run deposit insurance system, as does providing government financial support.

creditors.[35] But where it is less assured of being made whole, it may be unwilling to provide needed liquidity assistance even when appropriate. Similarly, the responsibilities of the supervisor or the ministry of finance may sometimes conflict with those of the deposit insurance system, so there can be advantages to housing them in separate agencies.

Accountability

A privately run and completely privately funded deposit insurance system is responsible to its member banks. While the government-run deposit insurance agency must be free from political interference and industry domination, it must be held accountable to the government, the public, and the banking industry for its decisions and actions. Otherwise, there is a greater risk that it would act in an arbitrary, capricious, or ineffectual manner. The path of accountability will differ depending on the political structure of the country and may well differ in a parliamentary system from a country that practices the separation of powers. Recommendations for facilitating accountability in a parliamentary system follow:

- The accountability of a government-run deposit insurance agency should be to the administration and to the legislature. Because the ministry of finance must ultimately meet the cost of any financial inadequacy in the authority fund, the agency might first be accountable to the ministry of finance. Through the ministry, the agency will be accountable to the cabinet, parliament, and, ultimately, to the public. The press will have an important role to play in keeping the public informed.

- The deposit insurance authority should be fiscally responsible, have financial integrity, and provide the public and the banking industry with a means of monitoring its performance. The authority must maintain its books and records in a transparent way and be subject to the same audit rules as other public entities. The records of a public deposit insurance agency must, therefore, be subject to a published annual audit conducted by the Office of the Auditor General or its equivalent.

Striking a Balance Between Independence and Accountability

Special arrangements are needed to strike an appropriate balance between independence and accountability. This can be achieved in a privately financed and privately run corporation by having bankers dominate the deposit insurance system's board. The board could be elected by the shareholders so as to represent all segments of the insured industry and not just the largest members. This should help to make the system politically independent (as long as it is financially sound and does not need to request financial support from the government). Having members elect the board for a fixed term of office, and having the board report to the members in an annual report and shareholders' meeting, encourages accountability.

Achieving the right balance is more problematic in a scheme that has government financial support and is run by a government agency/corporation. Political interference can be discouraged by making the deposit insurer a department of either the central bank or the supervisory agency, where the host has a constitution that grants it independence and a reputation supports it. But this arrangement can present conflicts of interest within the central bank or supervisory host. A number of countries prefer, therefore, to have a system that is separate from both the central bank and the supervisory agency. To gain independence it will need an appropriate implementing statute; adequate sources of private funding with legislated back-up funding that does not require parliamentary approval; fixed terms of office for members of the board who should be removed only for good and specified causes; clear criteria for eligibility for membership of the board;[36] an appointment process that features public hearings and legislative approval of the government nominee; and direct reporting of the deposit insurance system to parliament rather than to a government ministry.[37] In addition, an active and inquisitive press will facilitate accountability.

Staffing

The proposed deposit insurance agency could have a small staff in a country where there is not a large number of insured institutions and failures are rare. It can, in addition, delegate responsibilities to the central bank or the supervisory authority when necessary. Where the authority has a broad mandate, it could subcontract liquidations to private liquidators or financial institutions. Staff would need to be augmented in times of stress on the banking system

---

[35]U.S. congressional staff found that 90 percent of the extended credit granted by the U.S. Federal Reserve as lender of last resort went to banks that subsequently failed (U.S. House of Representatives, 1991, p. 94).

[36]Members of parliament or people currently employed in the industry should be ineligible.

[37]Having the deposit insurance system board report to the central bank or supervisory host is an alternative way to achieve independence, but it does so at the expense of accountability to the public.

by borrowing from the central bank or supervisor that had qualified personnel. Under the deposit insurance law, the staff (as well as the board) of the government-run authority must be granted legal protection in the form of immunities and protection against lawsuits for any actions they take in the course of their duties, and that are in accordance with the law. Staff would, of course, need analytical skills and high integrity.

Infrastructure

To support a system of deposit insurance, appropriate laws and an effective judicial system must be in place, so that property rights can be protected when needed. In addition, systems of accounting and auditing need to meet international standards to facilitate the accurate valuation of banks' portfolios. A broadly based financial system that includes, for example, insurance companies, will strengthen the banking system by allowing it to diversify its portfolios.

Public Relations

A good program of public relations will help maintain the credibility of the system of deposit protection. Such a program requires that the deposit insurer issue pamphlets and publications that keep the public informed about coverage under the guarantee. The public needs to know the monetary limits on coverage. These issues are easier for the public to understand and remember if they do not change frequently. The authority must also ensure that member institutions provide information on coverage to customers and potential customers. This will be easier if the deposit insurance system has its own logo, which members can display. The authority must also prevent nonmembers from masquerading as insured under the system.

Ensuring Financial Integrity

A number of financial issues need to be resolved before setting up a system: when to initiate the system of deposit insurance; whether to fund the system by ex ante premiums or ex post assessments on member institutions; where to set the target level for the fund; who should pay the start-up assessments; how to set the structure for premiums, provide back-up funding, and manage fund assets; and what should be the order of priority over the assets of a failed bank. Resolving these issues effectively will improve the financial position of the system and reduce its need to call on government resources for backup.

As mentioned previously, a deposit insurance system should be initiated when the banking system is sound. To do otherwise is to risk placing excessive demands on the fund before it has accumulated sufficient reserves; in such a case a crisis might drain the fund's coffers and result in its insolvency.[38]

To Fund Ex Ante or Ex Post?

Deposit insurance outlays can be met either from a fund that has been accumulated from system premiums paid in the past or by imposing an ex post levy assessed on surviving banks. In principle and in practice, it is possible to both accumulate a fund and to impose an additional levy ex post, if the fund proves to be insufficient. In fact, more countries have opted to build a fund ex ante, rather than to levy an ex post assessment (see Table A4 of the Statistical Appendix) and a number do "top up" their fund with additional ex post assessments, when the fund comes under financial pressure.[39] In either case, making it clear that the responsibility for covering the insured deposits of failed banks falls on banks, not the government, encourages banks to restrain their risk-prone peers, and thus reduces outlays by the system.

With regard to funding, it is recommended that:
- An insurance fund should be established. Most countries that have recently adopted a system of deposit insurance have established such a fund. An appropriate fund increases the flexibility to deal with banking problems and, thus, enhances public confidence in the deposit insurance and the banking systems.
- A country should choose a target level for its fund sufficient to cover outlays under normal circumstances. The target is often set as a percentage of insured deposits at a level that would enable the fund to cover insured depositors in a number of small banks, or say, two medium-sized banks or one large bank. It may need to be acknowledged that it would be too costly to maintain a fund at a level to enable a payout of all the deposits of the largest banks.[40] The deposit insurance agency would only be able to deal with problems in individual banks. In the case of a systemic crisis, the government would probably need to override the agency frame-

---

[38]The Bank Insurance Fund started in the United States after the banking system had been restructured by the Reconstruction Finance Corporation during the Great Depression. After accumulating a fund of $18 billion (or 1.25 percent of insured deposits) over the intervening years, the fund became illiquid, but not insolvent, in 1991 when faced by a large number of bank failures.

[39]Ex post assessments tend to be chosen by privately financed and privately operated deposit insurance scheme.

[40]Failure of a country's largest banks would be a systemic failure, as discussed in Section III.

work and adopt more comprehensive measures (see, for example, Enoch, Garcia, and Sundararajan, 1999).

Optimum Fund Size

Providing an analytical basis for determining the optimum size of a deposit insurance fund in any country is a subject where additional research is needed. There are two separate philosophies regarding fund size. One aims to have a fund large enough to self-sufficiently compensate depositors immediately when bank failures occur in normal times. The second philosophy is to reduce fund size, but only to a level that enables the system to borrow to pay depositors in failed banks. The system will then repay the borrowings over time. The second approach verges on ex post funding. The United States maintain a large fund; Canada a smaller fund.

Start-Up Funding

A newly established system may receive initial contributions from banks, the government, and/or the central bank (Table A4 of the Statistical Appendix). Where banks are strong enough initially to foot the bill, they should do so. But this is often not the case.

Whatever its source:
- *Initial funding* should be set at a level sufficient to make the scheme credible and operational. As the scheme will ideally be introduced only when the banking system is sound, the scheme should not have to handle any failures upon its introduction. Nevertheless, the initial contribution should be sufficient to enable the fund to reach its full target capitalization as quickly as possible.
- If the government provides initial funding, provision can be made for the deposit insurance fund or banks to repay the government's contribution over time.

Ongoing Funding—Premiums

Going forward, an insurance fund would be accumulated and members would be required to pay premiums quarterly or semiannually at the rate of "x" percent per year based on total deposits. The premiums would be levied as needed to cover expenses and build, maintain, or rebuild the fund to its target level. Thus, premiums will vary from country to country and from time to time. Levying premiums on all kinds of deposits (insured and uninsured) is easier to administer, and it provides a broader contribution base, although many countries find it more equitable to levy charges against only the total value of deposits held in insurable instruments, or to go further toward equity and levy only against the value

of those deposits that are actually covered (for country practices in this regard, see Table A4 of the Statistical Appendix).

When setting premiums, policymakers should keep the following in mind:
- Regular premiums or contributions should be set by the deposit insurance agency as a percentage of total, insurable, or insured deposits. An argument can be made that premiums should be assessed on all deposits, because all depositors, whether insured or not, benefit from the system of deposit insurance. A number of countries, however, believe that fairness is enhanced by confining assessment to insured deposits—that is, those who benefit most directly.
- Premiums could be paid directly to the deposit insurance agency or they could be automatically deducted by the central bank from the reserve accounts of members and passed to the system.
- Premium levels will vary with the deposit base. The broader the base, the lower is the premium necessary to achieve a chosen income level. The premium could be determined by the deposit insurance agency, but should not exceed a legally set rate that would impose an undue burden on covered institutions.
- The agency's board would have the discretion to reduce premiums but only after the target level for the fund is reached, and after the initial contribution by the government has been repaid. The premium reduction should be made in a way that maintains the fund at its target level.
- The board should have the right to levy additional premiums if the fund has been depleted. These premiums would continue until the fund is restored to desired levels.
- Bankers should be encouraged when they recognize that premiums will be reduced once the fund reaches its target. They would then have incentives to support early intervention by supervisors in problem banks to limit future claims on the fund.
- Risk-based premiums are fairer in principle and should reward sound institutions. Premiums should be set at a uniform (flat) rate, however, until the supervisory system is in a good position to differentiate among risk profiles. Otherwise, bankers will contest those assessments they perceive to be unfair. Once the supervisors have honed their monitoring and assessment capabilities, a system of risk-based premiums can be introduced, preferably one that reduces the premium for exceptionally strong banks, while raising it for risky institutions.
- Premiums would be accounted for as an expense and thus would be tax deductible. They would not be counted as an asset of the con-

tributing institution. Paying premiums would be the legal obligation of each institution, and a cost of doing banking business in the country. As such, the expense should be tax-deductible.

Controlling Outlays

To preserve fund levels and keep premiums low, the insurer needs to restrict its outlays through efficient operations, maximize recoveries from the disposition of the assets of failed banks, limit its obligations in various ways, and make wise investments. Dealing with troubled banks promptly and firmly reduces outlays.

Depositor Preference

Giving depositors and/or the insurance fund preference over the assets of the failed bank increases their share in the value recovered and reduces the fund's net outlays, while increasing the share of the losses borne by others (Garcia 1996, Appendix I).

In the absence of deposit insurance, the treatment of depositors, creditors, and other claimants when a bank fails is determined by the priorities that the law establishes among claimants over the assets of the bank in liquidation. Deposit insurance, in effect, satisfies small depositors' claims first. It must therefore be determined where the deposit insurer itself stands within the hierarchy of claimants.

One way to protect the resources of the deposit insurance system is to give depositors, or the system itself, priority over the claims on the assets of the insured failed bank. Such priority has an advantage in that it increases the amount the system is likely to recover from the failed bank's assets, and so reduces financial demands on the accumulated fund. The more the system recovers, the less it has to call on its accumulated resources or levy its members. But priority also has a major disadvantage where the insurer is the receiver/liquidator of the failed bank. It then has less, or no, incentive to maximize the total value of recovered assets, especially in cases where it has a legal priority. If depositors, insured depositors, or the system itself are reimbursed ahead of other claimants, they will receive a higher proportion on all of their claims than they would, absent such priority. Granting priority conserves fund resources, but it does so at the expense of other claimants and it may reduce the care that the deposit insurance system executes when it liquidates or otherwise disposes of the assets of the failed bank.

The choice between granting priority and not granting it (i.e., having the deposit insurer, succeeding to the rights of the insured depositors, with the same priority over the assets of a failed institution as large depositors, and ranking equally with general (unsecured) creditors) is a judgment call. The choice would be influenced by an assessment of the balance between a fiscal need and deposit insurance system efficiency in recoveries. This recommendation would need to be coordinated with the priorities established in new Banking and Bankruptcy Laws.

Managing Fund Assets

Another defense of the fund is to invest fund resources wisely, preferably in safe assets. As even government paper may not always be sufficiently liquid in a small volatile economy, the deposit insurance system may wish to invest in government securities abroad. It should not place deposits in troubled banks.[41]

When investing fund resources:

- The deposit insurance agency fund should be invested in government securities. The agency should not be allowed to invest in risky securities or investments that might cause a loss. Funds should *not* be placed as deposits in insured institutions. The insurance fund should earn market interest on the funds it has accumulated and carefully consider its needs for liquidity. Government securities are an appropriate investment and safe haven for the agency fund. The agency should determine the most appropriate maturity for those securities. For example, the securities could be long-term because longer maturities would typically pay higher interest rates. Safety, however, is of greater importance than yield. The fund should be able to discount its government securities at the central bank to get liquidity when needed. Investing in (sound) foreign government securities may diversify the portfolio, protect against foreign exchange losses, and against credit risk if the financial position of the domestic government is weak.

Back-Up Funding

Despite the efforts to build a fund and control expenses, in times of stress, the accumulated fund may prove insufficient to meet the demands placed upon it. For example, unexpected failures could impose more costs than the deposit insurance agency had an-

---

[41]Venezuela's deposit insurance reserves were invested heavily in insolvent banks, whereas they should have been invested in safe assets that can be easily liquidated in case of a need. This typically means investing in government securities at home or abroad. Small countries, in particular, may wish to diversify by investing fund resources in easily marketable securities issued by foreign governments to keep the fund liquid and protect its value against high rates of inflation. Investing in foreign government securities would give some protection against foreign exchange losses in highly dollarized economies.

ticipated. The system will need back-up sources of funding to cover this contingency. It could have a government guarantee, a right to borrow without limit from the treasury/the national debt office, the central bank, or from the markets.[42] In addition, the deposit insurer might purchase reinsurance coverage from private insurance companies, although such companies typically do not have resources that are adequate to cover systemic banking problems. As indicated above, provisions should be made for the government to cover shortfalls in the fund by, for example, imposing an ex post levy or additional insurance premiums stretched over time. This provision will reduce the impact of the system's demands on the budget in the longer term and will enhance financial stability and fiscal sustainability. Partly because the central bank has very limited capital of its own, IMF staff have generally recommended that the government, not the central bank, support a system, although a central bank may provide temporary lender-of-last-resort support to a system with a government guarantee.[43]

The Government Guarantee

The following points should be considered when a government guarantees the deposit insurance agency:

- The government's explicit and irrevocable guarantee should be provided under the law that establishes the deposit insurance agency. The fund may need a government guarantee to be credible with the public. If banking supervision is strengthened and the agency is properly managed, there should never be any reason to activate this guarantee.
- To maintain the credibility of the system, the agency should have the power to borrow according to rules but without any limit on the amount needed to restore its viability from the treasury/debt agency or the central bank and issue bonds and notes in the markets. The agency would have no authority to take a loan from any other financial institution. The agency could need to borrow if it were to have insufficient resources to pay out or transfer deposits. It could be illiquid but solvent, because it had invested in long-term government securities for which there may not be a liquid market. In this

situation, it could discount its assets or borrow against its assets from the central bank. It could also be allowed to borrow from the markets.

- The agency would not need to provide good collateral against loans from the central bank where it has full government backing. (The central banking act should reflect this recommendation.) The government's guarantee of the deposit insurance system would ensure that any central bank liquidity support is repaid. The agency would not need prior approval from the ministry of finance to borrow from the central bank.
- The deposit insurance agency would need to seek prior approval (from the ministry of finance and central bank) regarding the timing of borrowing from the markets. Given the government guarantee, the agency should be required to seek prior approval from the ministry of finance for any borrowing in the markets, to avoid a situation where such borrowing would conflict with the timing of other government issues or with the objectives of monetary management.
- The agency should have the authority to impose special, additional, ex post assessments on all member institutions, as needed; for example, to repay borrowed funds. The law should specify a limit to the combined assessments that could be imposed on banks in any one year. For example, analysis might reveal that it would be unwise to let the sum of regular and special assessments exceed 1 or 2 percent of total deposits in any one year. However, although the industry would not have the capacity to pay an unlimited amount in any one year, special assessments could be repeated until borrowed funds are repaid.

A Summary of IMF Advice

The recommendations above seek to create an incentive-compatible system of deposit protection to keep the banking system sound and to avert crises. A properly designed system of deposit protection can help underpin the stability of the system while limiting government outlays, if it is introduced (1) in situations of reasonably solvent (possibly restructured) banks; (2) with the support of adequate prudential regulation and supervision; and (3) if accompanied by well-formulated lender-of-last-resort policies by the central bank or others.[44] The severe problems in the U.S. savings and loan industry in the 1980s demonstrated that a poorly designed deposit insurance system can weaken internal controls, thwart

---

[42]Funds raised in the national debt markets are monetarily neutral, which is important where bank solvency is a problem.

[43]Central banks typically have very little capital and no power to tax; therefore, all too frequently, the only way to cover any losses they incur is to print money. From a fiscal perspective, the accounts of the central bank and the government should be consolidated; although the budget effects of lender-of-last-resort and deposit insurance system losses are often hidden as "quasi-fiscal" losses at the central bank.

[44]Having a currency board forced Argentina to use alternative means to support illiquid banks.

market discipline, and hamper supervisory action. Consequently, good design is important. While a weak incentive structure will not necessarily make a system insolvent, it may lead to higher premiums or additional supervision and regulation, both of which will be opposed by the banking community as limiting the growth of their industry.

The IMF has advised that deposit insurance can assist in the maintenance of a stable system, but only if it is accompanied by an effective system of supervision and clear legislation, including firm entry and exit policies. An efficient and competitive banking system should allow for entry of new banks (that are adequately capitalized and have fit and proper owners and managers) and, more important, should force the early exit of nonviable and insolvent banks whose presence can distort competition and lead to a rapid buildup of losses.[45] The legal and supervisory framework should allow for a spectrum of prompt corrective actions to restore troubled banks to health, or facilitate their resolution in order to keep individual insolvencies from developing into systemic unsoundness. However, prompt exit reduces the losses

that are incurred and is facilitated by formal provisions that protect small depositors from loss. Such protection helps to avoid the public complaints and political pressures that often accompany the closing of uninsured banks. Fears of public outcry have sometimes persuaded officials to keep troubled banks operating unresolved until runs occur.

IMF advice has cautioned that, as far as possible, deposit insurance should not be introduced in situations where banks are widely believed to be insolvent and where banking supervision is inadequate. The reason is that in such situations, the government will be tempted to give depositors a comprehensive guarantee that will be very expensive for it to underwrite and that it may not have the means to support. In addition, such a full guarantee may reward those who allowed the banking problems to occur in the first place. An additional problem is that it may allow the authorities to avoid taking the measures that are needed to strengthen the system, and so set the stage for a repetition of problems in the future.

With or without a system of deposit insurance, despite all precautions, careful design and implementation of the system, mistakes may be made and/or contagion can bring a banking crisis even to well-prepared countries. In that event, additional measures that are discussed in Section IV may become necessary.

---

[45]While a discussion of viable and nonviable banks is beyond the scope of this paper, a viable bank is one that has enough earning assets in relation to liabilities to be profitable enough to rebuild capital to acceptable levels over a short time (two- to three-year) horizon. See Lindgren, Garcia, and Saal (1996).

III   A Survey of Deposit Insurance Practices

A recent survey of 85 different systems of deposit protection found that of the 85, 67 countries offered an explicit, limited deposit insurance system in normal times (see Table A1 of the Statistical Appendix).[46] They are the focus of the survey that follows.[47] As Table 2 shows, four of the surveyed countries are in Africa, 10 are in Asia, 32 are in Europe, four are in the Middle East, and 17 are in the Americas.

Year of Origin of Limited Deposit Insurance Systems

Although two of the three systems in the United States (one for commercial banks and the second for savings associations) were started in the 1930s, it was not until the 1960s that other countries began to adopt the deposit insurance systems that are still in existence.[48] Eight schemes were initiated in the 1960s, and nine in the 1970s. As the incidence of banking crises escalated in the 1980s, 19 schemes were initiated during the decade. Thirty new limited systems commenced during the 1990s, as banking problems continued to escalate on all continents. (See Figure 2).

Revisions to deposit insurance systems have been quite common, especially since the European Union Directive in 1994.[49]

The survey, whose results are presented in the Statistical Appendix tables, will be used to throw some light on common practices. Later, the survey will also be used to examine the extent to which good practices have been adopted, and where they have been disregarded.[50] It finds that countries are increasingly adopting provisions that temper incentive problems, but certain deficiencies remain in some instances.

The Deposit Insurance Agency: Role and Responsibilities

There are basically two models for the role and responsibilities of a deposit insurance agency. Under a narrow construction, the deposit insurance system's obligation is to pay depositors of failed banks when instructed to do so by the appropriate authority, which is frequently the bank supervisor, and to acquire the funds by collecting premiums and building a fund or by imposing ex post assessments. The deposit insurance agency in 34 countries plays such a narrow role. The alternative model for the agency is much more comprehensive. The agency takes charge of failed banks and resolves them according to the country's laws. The deposit insurance agency in 33 countries carries a broad range of responsibilities that often includes anticipating bank problems and resolving failed banks. The narrow construction dominates in Europe, but broader responsibilities are common in Asia and the Western Hemisphere. Moreover, a number of countries have recently broadened the role for their agencies or they are considering enlarging those responsibilities. None is known to be considering reducing that role.

Membership

Table A1 of the Statistical Appendix shows that, to avoid the problem of adverse selection, 62 of the

---

[46]Seventy-two countries had systems that were explicitly defined in law and/or regulation. Full coverage was being offered in Spring 2000 in 10 of these countries. In seven of the full-coverage cases, comprehensive coverage replaces systems that have limited scope in normal times. Six African countries that have not fully ratified their agreement to form a regional insurance system and the system in Panama are excluded from the survey because it applies the guarantee only to credit cooperatives. Russia is also excluded because of a dearth of information.

[47]The entries in the Tables A1 through A7 of the Statistical Appendix extend and update into the second quarter of 2000 the survey results presented in Garcia (1999), which were exhaustively reviewed. Every effort has been made to include new schemes in the tables and to reflect revisions that have been made to existing schemes. The author requests the reader's forgiveness if any changes have been missed, because changes are frequent at present.

[48]Some states within the United States began a deposit insurance system earlier, as did the former Czechoslovakia.

[49]In addition to the revisions included in the Statistical Appendix, the United Kingdom expected to revise its system before long.

---

[50]Issues relating to prompt corrective action, failure resolution, and speed of depositor compensation were not surveyed.

Table 2. Countries with Explicit, Limited Deposit Insurance Systems

Africa (4)	Asia (10)	Europe (32)		Middle East (4)	Western Hemisphere (17)
Kenya	Bangladesh	Austria	Latvia	Bahrain	Argentina
Nigeria	India	Belgium	Lithuania	Lebanon	Barbados
Tanzania	Japan	Bulgaria	Luxembourg	Morocco	Brazil
Uganda	Kazakhstan	Croatia	Macedonia	Oman	Canada
	Korea	Czech Rep.	Netherlands		Chile
	Marshall Islands	Denmark	Norway		Colombia
	Micronesia	Estonia	Poland		Dominican Republic
	Philippines	Finland	Portugal		Ecuador
	Sri Lanka	France	Romania		El Salvador
	Taiwan Province of China	Germany	Slovak Rep.		Guatemala
		Gibraltar	Spain		Honduras
		Greece	Sweden		Jamaica
		Hungary	Switzerland		Mexico
		Iceland	Turkey		Peru
		Ireland	Ukraine		Trinidad & Tobago
		Italy	United Kingdom		United States
					Venezuela

Source: Survey results presented in Table A7 of the Statistical Appendix.

Figure 2. Decade of Origination of Explicit Deposit Insurance Systems
(Number of Countries)

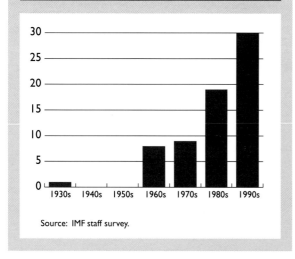

Source: IMF staff survey.

systems surveyed are compulsory.[51] Nevertheless, seven schemes are voluntary and three of the voluntary schemes (those in the Dominican Republic, Sri Lanka, and Switzerland) do not impose risk-adjusted premiums as an alternative means to combat adverse selection.[52]

While objectives are not investigated by the survey, they can sometimes be inferred from deposit insurance practices. For example, if the objective of the system is primarily to protect small depositors, a country is likely to include all institutions that are licensed to accept deposits (particularly, small deposits) from the public. To reduce unfairness to well-supervised institutions, the country makes an effort to oversee all insured institutions to the same strict standards. But, where a country is more interested in maintaining financial stability, it may confine membership to those classes of institution that it considers to have systemic importance. In this case, membership may be focused principally on commercial banks. There may also be subsidiary insurance schemes for smaller, or less systematically important groups of institutions, such as savings associations and credit cooperatives.

Table A2 of the Statistical Appendix examines these issues and finds that countries typically attempt to cover (in one or more insurance system) all institutions that take deposits. Confining coverage to licensed commercial banks tends to be the exception, not the general rule (column 2, Table A3).

---

[51]The sum of the numbers of compulsory and voluntary systems exceeds 67 because some countries have more than one deposit insurance system.

[52]The voluntary system in Sri Lanka began in 1987 by charging its 13 members a premium of 0.04 percent of deposits. In 1992, the premium was raised to 0.15 percent and two banks withdrew. Only seven members currently remain.

Countries typically require the branches and subsidiaries of foreign banks that are operating (taking small deposits) within a country to belong to the system (column 3, Table A2). Countries in the European Union may relax this requirement somewhat by granting exemptions to foreign institutions that are covered by their home system of deposit insurance, although they may allow them to join if coverage in the host country's system is more generous than the home scheme. Country authorities typically see their responsibility to protect their citizens. Thus, they typically do not insure the deposits that domestic banks take offshore (column 4, Table A2). The survey noted two exceptions to this general practice. The first covers countries of the European Union, which often offer coverage to customers of their banks anywhere within the European Union. The second exception is countries that are particularly dependent on foreign deposits and fear the impact of their loss on the domestic financial system.

Funding the Deposit Insurance System

Funding for the system of deposit insurance has to be adequate, and has to be seen by the public to be sufficient, if the system is to succeed in compensating depositors and maintaining public confidence. To this end, there are a number of issues to be addressed. They include whether (1) funding should be mainly private, but have public backing in emergencies; (2) the system should accumulate a fund or impose ex post levies; and (3) whether to give to depositors or the insurance system legal priority over the assets of the failed bank.

Private Funding

A deposit insurance system that is privately funded encourages bankers to keep their institutions sound. All but one of the 67 of the explicit, limited systems in the survey are privately funded by their member institutions. Only Chile offers an exception; its system is fully funded by the government.

Official Backing

As discussed in Section II, an underfunded scheme will prove to be an obstacle to closing failed banks and so may lead to costly forbearance.[53] Countries usually decide that they want the govern-

ment to back up a well-run system of deposit insurance that is met by unexpected demands on its resources and is in need of additional funds in order to carry out its responsibilities. Consequently, many countries make provisions for the government (preferably, but not always through the ministry of finance) to assist a depleted fund with loans. While 66 of the explicit, limited systems have private funding, 55 have access to public funding. Some have already received financial help from official sources to get the system started or to cope with a systemic banking crisis; others expect to obtain it when they need assistance (column 3, Table A3). To contain moral hazard among bankers, banks must be required to repay their loans, including those from the government.

The Canadian government goes further in requiring that the Canada Deposit Insurance Corporation (CDIC) pay a "credit enhancement fee" to the government when it borrows funds in the private markets. The rationale is that, as a Crown Corporation, the CDIC can borrow at a lower rate than it would if it were a private corporation. The fee covers the difference. Thus, when the CDIC borrows it pays a private market rate.

As mentioned in the discussion of good practices, a reticence to commit public funds would be understandable where a deposit insurance scheme is privately run because of potential conflicts of interest. The information in two of the tables in the Statistical Appendix (Tables A4 and A8) brings to light cases where such conflicts of interest may exist among ex post systems. The two tables show that seven of the privately administered ex post systems do have access to back-up funding from the government. In two other instances, however, the authorities explicitly deny that they offer backup funding. The situation is unspecified and unclear in the other three instances. Only one ex post system (in the Netherlands) is operated by the government.

Ex Post Schemes and Funded Deposit Insurance Schemes

A country has a choice between funding its system of deposit insurance ex ante by regularly charging premiums to member banks and accumulating them in a fund, or imposing a levy on surviving member institutions after a member bank fails. As shown in column 4 of Table A3, most (58) countries have opted for a funded system.

However, nine countries—Austria, Bahrain, Germany (for its private system), Gibraltar, Italy, Luxembourg, the Netherlands, Switzerland, and the United Kingdom—fund their systems solely or mainly by imposing a levy on members after a bank fails and its depositors need to be compensated. Ex

---

[53]The best known example of an insolvent insurance scheme is perhaps the Federal Savings and Loan Insurance Corporation in the United States, which practiced forbearance for a number of years with costly consequences for U.S. taxpayers.

post funding is more popular in Western Europe than elsewhere. That popularity is waning, however; Germany instituted a government-run funded scheme in 1998, France changed from an ex post to a funded system in 1999, Bahrain has draft legislation to fund its system, and Italy is reported to be considering switching to a funded system.

Contrasting Ex Post and Funded Deposit Insurance Systems

Differences need not be inherent in the design of the two different forms of deposit insurance systems; but in practice, they exist. There are, in fact, a number of differences—some important—between funded and most ex post systems.[54] First, five of the ex post schemes began in Europe in the late 1970s and early 1980s, which is earlier than many of the funded schemes.[55] Second, ex post schemes were often initiated by groups of bankers seeking mutual protection, whereas funded insurance systems have more typically been sponsored by the government. Third, seven of the ex post systems have remained both privately funded and administered. (Bahrain's and Gibraltar's privately funded systems are jointly administered.) Four of the ex post, privately administered schemes have government backing, however—a situation that presents potential conflicts of interest.

Funded schemes appear to be more rule-based and offer less discretion for the administrators and less uncertainty for those insured than ex post systems. The reason may be that ex post systems are privately run by their member institutions and they lack the authority of a government agency to promulgate and enforce rules. So, typically, private systems have not transparently specified members' responsibilities regarding sharing the costs of compensating depositors. They also often lack backstop funding from the government; are limited in their roles and responsibilities; and, because they are privately run, have difficulty in obtaining information from the supervisor and the central bank. Given that good practices recommend transparency and sharing information, it is perhaps not surprising that most recently created systems have opted to build a government-sponsored fund.

One of the notable ambiguities in ex post systems concerns the base on which the insurance obligation is to be calculated. While four ex post countries base the insurance obligation on insured deposits and another uses total deposits, the base is less specific in Germany's private schemes, Italy, the Netherlands, and Switzerland (Table A4).

One of the principal differences between ex post and funded systems is in the coverage they offer. Ex post schemes typically offer low coverage. For example, Austria, Luxembourg, the Netherlands, Switzerland, and Bahrain all offer coverage at less than per capita GDP (see Figure 1). Only Italy (at 5.5 times per capita GDP) and Germany's private system offer coverage above the commonly used rule-of-thumb of twice per capita GDP. In addition, Austria (for business deposits), Gibraltar, Luxembourg, and the United Kingdom also impose a haircut on deposits under their systems of coinsurance.

There is likely to be a difficulty for a government-run central bank or supervisory agency to pass confidential information on financial condition of a member bank to a privately run bankers' club that is operating an insurance system. Deposit insurance staff in Argentina and France have explicitly mentioned this difficulty. Germany's private system requires its members to be audited and classified by the Auditing Association of German Banks, which can impose disciplinary measures.

Guarding Fund Resources

Investing fund assets wisely will guard fund resources. The survey noted—in column 5 of Table A3—that many systems place their resources in domestic government securities. Some encourage investment in safe assets abroad. Unfortunately, a number of deposit insurance systems invest their funds in domestic banks, which places them in jeopardy.

Granting Depositors or the Deposit Insurance System/Deposit Insurance Agency Legal Priority

From their actions, half of the countries surveyed (where information was available) perceive the fiscal advantages of giving depositors priority over a failed bank's assets to be more important than the incentive risks. The other half assess the balance differently. Table A3, column 6, shows that 31 of the countries surveyed gave legal priority to depositors or the deposit insurer, but 30 countries did not. In other countries, such as Hong Kong SAR and Malaysia, priority is/was used as a way to protect

---

[54]The author is grateful to Charles Siegman for this insight.

[55]Initially, a number of the ex post schemes were voluntary, but by the end of the twentieth century all were compulsory. All but one (Bahrain) of the nine ex post systems are located in Europe and all but two of the European ex post insurance systems (Gibraltar and Switzerland) belong to countries that are members of the European Union. The EU Directive on Deposit Guarantee Schemes requires member countries to offer compulsory deposit insurance. Consequently, two member countries (Germany and Italy) with ex post schemes that were previously voluntary now offer compulsory systems of deposit insurance. In addition, France switched from a voluntary, ex post system to a compulsory funded scheme in mid-1999. As a result, today, both funded and ex post schemes are now typically mandatory.

depositors without establishing a formal system. (Malaysia found legal priority insufficient on its own to maintain depositor confidence during the Asian crisis and also introduced an explicit full guarantee. Hong Kong SAR is considering introducing a limited system of deposit insurance.)[56]

Choosing When to Begin

A country must make an important decision regarding when to introduce a deposit insurance scheme. Beginning one too soon before the banking system has been strengthened can lead to risky behavior at weak banks that will lead to major expenditures in resolving failed banks and can cause the system to become insolvent. Yet, countries are often tempted to begin a limited, explicit system when a crisis is imminent or in progress in the mistaken belief that it will avoid or cure the crisis. Limited coverage will not prevent uninsured depositors from running to safer havens. Even without a systemic crisis but fearing runs, the authorities may consider setting the coverage rate high—perhaps too high.

If the public perceives that all banks are weak, there is a risk of a "flight from the system and from the currency" to banks abroad. Otherwise, there will be a flight "to quality" from weak banks to safer institutions within the country. Only full coverage can (but not necessarily will) counter flights to quality and from the currency. Thus, to initiate a limited deposit insurance system when there is a risk of deposit runs, is to invite such runs. Setting high, but limited, coverage does not resolve the dilemma. Not only may there be runs by those depositors who hold deposits above the limit; but politically, later reducing the coverage level in order to reduce moral hazard will prove very difficult.[57] Faced with a systemic crisis, a country has two main courses of action to avoid runs: retain its existing implicit guarantee; or institute a full, explicit, temporary guarantee. Questions concerning the placement of a full guarantee and its removal are addressed in more detail in Section IV.

Controlling Administrative Costs

Limiting administrative costs is an additional way to protect system resources. The staff may be kept small, but may be supplemented in emergencies by borrowing skilled employees from other agencies. The scheme (particularly a narrow system of deposit insurance) may also be managed by another agency, where it would remain largely dormant until needed. While the survey did not inquire systematically into such practices, column 6 of Table A8 of the Statistical Appendix provides some information on country practices with regard to running the deposit insurance scheme.

Setting a Target for the Fund

Many countries find it useful for the deposit insurance agency to set a target level for the fund (usually expressed as a percentage of total or insured deposits) that would allow it to attain and retain financial viability and avoid the financial deficiencies that lead to forbearance for troubled banks and/or insolvency of the fund. Private funding needs to be sufficient to meet all demands that can be expected to be placed upon it in normal times and in moderately adverse circumstances. When the insurance system is new, the target will be initially set after forecasting the income and expenses (including outlays to compensate depositors of failed banks) of the fund. The target then provides an indication of the premiums that need to be set, and subsequently whether they should be reduced when the fund exceeds its target level, or raised to replenish a depleted fund. Setting an appropriate target demands a realistic assessment of the condition of the banking industry, the size and timing of the financial demands that are likely to be placed on the fund, the system's ability to borrow when necessary, and the industry's ability to pay the necessary premiums without prejudicing its profitability, solvency, and liquidity.[58]

Canada has adopted a different approach. It requires its system to estimate its future losses and to make provision for them. Such provisions form a part of the accumulated fund, which may not be sufficient to compensate depositors in the interval before the failed bank's assets are sold. Should the CDIC need liquidity or underestimate the demands that are placed upon it, it can borrow from the markets or the government to supplement its small fund. This process involves partial reliance on ex post funding to repay the borrowed funds.

Column 2 of Table A4 shows that 29 countries (most of which have a funded system) maintain a

---

[56]Among countries granting full guarantee (Costa Rica—for state-owned banks, Ecuador, Honduras, Indonesia, Japan, Korea, Malaysia, Mexico, Thailand, and Turkey), Ecuador, Malaysia, Mexico, and Turkey had previously granted depositors priority.

[57]Countries, such as the United States, set a high level when it raised coverage in 1980 and had to wait for inflation and the growth of GDP to reduce the coverage ratio to more incentive-compatible levels. The $100,000 limit set by the United States in 1980 was virtually nine times per capita GDP at that time. It has taken 19 years to reduce the coverage ratio to the current more incentive-compatible level of three times 1999 GDP. The excessively high coverage contributed to the S&L crisis in the 1980s. (See Garcia and Plautz, 1988, pages 257–279).

---

[58]If the banking industry is very weak, a deposit insurance scheme may not be feasible until it has been restructured.

Figure 3. Insurance Fund Targets and Actual Levels Attained

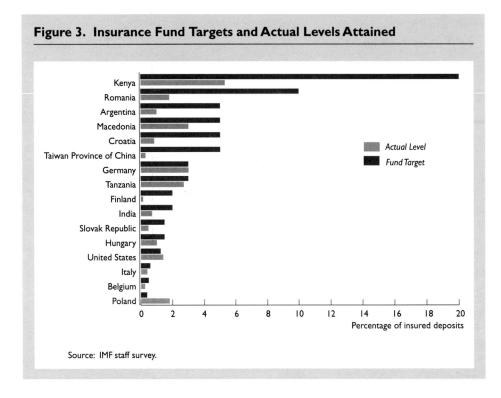

Source: IMF staff survey.

target level for the fund, which is often expressed as a desirable percentage of insured deposits. Eight have explicitly not set a target. Gibraltar, Italy, and the United Kingdom have small targets for covering administrative expenses in their ex post schemes, but small size does not reflect on the adequacy of the capital resources of the system in these countries. The target in funded systems ranges from a low of 0.4 percent of all deposits in Poland to the very high levels of 20 percent of insured deposits in Kenya, and an unrealistically high 50 percent in Ecuador. The level of accumulation actually achieved by most countries falls below the targeted level. Funding deficiencies are not universal, however. Ukraine reports a healthy balance of 10 percent of insured deposits in its fund, Tanzania approximates the target for its fund, and the United States' balance in its funds exceeds their targets. (Italy exceeded its low target for meeting administrative expenses until the fund recently became depleted by bank failures in the southern region). Figure 3 shows the varying targets to which countries aspire and the levels (expressed as a percentage of insured deposits) that they actually maintain.

The Premium Base

As deposits are the entity that is insured, most systems use deposits as the base on which to charge premiums or to calculate the levy needed to compen-

sate depositors under ex post assessments. Charging premiums on all of the deposits that a bank holds is easier to administer than to charge selectively. Twenty-seven countries do so, but many consider charging premiums on categories of deposits that are not eligible for insurance inequitable. Thirty-six countries, therefore, levy charges against insured deposits (Table A4, column 4).

Some systems (six) impose charges on the total value of deposits in those categories that are eligible for insurance. These are referred to as "insurable deposits" in Table A4. Seven others, such as Austria, Belgium, Canada, Guatemala, Sweden, Peru, and Taiwan Province of China, go farther and charge only for the amount of deposits that would be compensated if the bank were to fail. That is, premiums are paid on the sum of deposits that lie below the limit of coverage. That amount is referred to as "amount covered" in Table A4.

The latter procedure is more equitable in that it avoids this cross-subsidization of insured deposits by noninsured deposits, but it can be much more difficult to administer. In many cases, the information available (for example, the English translation of a country's deposit insurance law) was not sufficiently precise to determine whether premiums were charged on insured categories of deposits or only on the amount actually covered. These cases are listed as "insured deposits" in the table. Clearly, calculating correctly the amount of deposits actually insured involves knowing the size distribution of the deposits of each depositor in each insured bank. Not all countries collect the information necessary to make this calculation, especially on a regular basis.

A few countries use a base other than deposits. For example, Norway bases its charges on risk-adjusted assets. Poland charges premiums on deposits but sets an upper bound to those premiums that is based on risk-adjusted assets.

Premiums Levied

A scheme that relies on an accumulated fund will need to charge adequate premiums. Table A4 shows that 58 systems charge premiums at regular intervals. The size of the premium needed to maintain a healthy fund will depend on the current condition of the banking system and its future prospects. Premiums charged in 1999 ranged from a temporary zero percent of deposits for strong banks in the United States,[59] and a regular low of 0.005 percent in Bangladesh, and a high of 2 percent in Venezuela, which has experienced severe banking problems in the mid-1990s (see Table A4 of the Statistical Appendix). Figure 4 shows a distribution of premiums by size, and deposit base. The mode of the distribution is 0.15 percent and the medium lies in the band between 0.2 an 0.3 percent.

Without detailed knowledge of the condition of each country's banking system and deposit insurance system, judging whether the premiums being charged are adequate to cover immediate outlays or to accumulate a fund sufficient to survive the next banking crisis is difficult. However, it is noticeable that the actual level of the accumulated fund falls well below its target level in one-third of the 29 countries that maintain a target, suggesting that premiums in these countries are not currently adequate to meet the needs they face. Moreover, lax accounting permits systems in some countries to report misleadingly healthy levels of accumulated resources.[60] In addition, premiums in other countries that do not set a target may also be insufficient to cover the risks that the system faces.

Risk-Adjusting Premiums

Adjusting the premiums that banks pay for risk is conceptually a challenging process. In addition,

there are at least two practical problems to risk-adjusting the premiums banks pay for the deposit guarantee. Solving these problems may be expected to elicit country-specific responses.

The first problem is accurately forecasting the degree of risk that a bank places on the fund—it is a skill that is currently undeveloped. Moreover, the risk premiums imposed by the deposit insurance agency need to be based on objective criteria so that they can be justified to the bank and the courts, should the bank challenge the ruling. Two popular candidates for inclusion in the calculation of a bank's risk to the deposit insurance system are capital adequacy and supervisory rating. Some countries use one, some the other, while others, including the United States, combines capital adequacy and CAMELS rating into a composite measure. There are disadvantages to these measures, however. Capital adequacy, even when accurately measured, tends to be a lagging indicator of bank condition, and is also subject to manipulation through a bank's system of loan classification and provisioning. Although supervisory ratings are kept confidential in most countries, they will be revealed if the bank's annual accounts report the premium the bank is paying.[61] An alternative, more direct approach to risk-adjustment (used by Norway, Poland, and Germany's system for savings and cooperative banks) is to charge flat-rate premiums on risk-adjusted assets instead of deposits, so that banks with less risky assets pay less for their insurance.[62] This approach saves the banks some effort because they have already calculated the risk-adjusted assets in order to assess their capital adequacy. However, it may place undue emphasis on imprecisely measured risk-adjusted assets.

A number of other countries use a complex formula to assess risk (Argentina, Canada, Italy, Kazakhstan, Romania, and Taiwan Province of China). To retain confidentiality and track risk accurately, the calculation of the risk premium can be designed to be complex; yet there is a valid argument for simplicity, transparency, and accountability in premium setting. The just-mentioned characteristics may be desirable when the financial system is sound, but are unattainable when it is weak. Thus, countries may want to announce their intention to risk-adjust premiums and then set a timetable for successive stages of widening the premium band so that the banks have time to make complementary adjustments as they wish.

---

[59]By law, the Federal Deposit Insurance Corporation in the United States does not impose premiums on the highest quality banks when its fund is above its statutory target level of 1.25 percent of insured deposits, as it is in the year 2000.

[60]For example, a deposit insurance scheme may have made a financial assistance loan to a very weak bank that may not be repaid but allows the bank to keep operating. The system may not have made provision for the losses expected on this loan.

---

[61]The current proposal by the Basel Committee on Banking Supervision to allow supervisors to set institution-specific capital adequacy ratios would make it more difficult for the public to discover its supervisory rating.

[62]Poland also uses risk-based assets to provide an upper bound on premiums that are, in practice, determined as a percentage of total deposits.

Figure 4. Premiums on Total Deposits, Insurable Deposits, and Covered Deposits

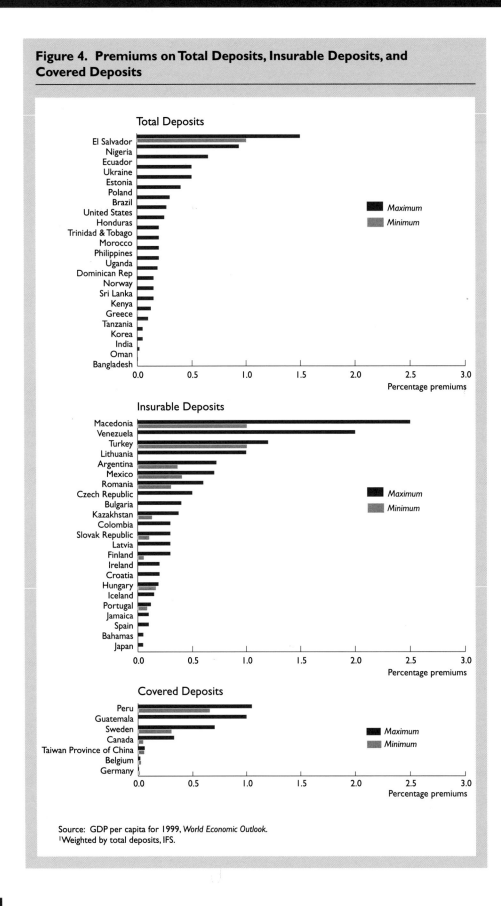

Source: GDP per capita for 1999, *World Economic Outlook.*
[1]Weighted by total deposits, IFS.

The second problem is that a degree of subsidy is inherent in insurance. If premiums were to precisely represent a bank's risk to the fund, they would become prohibitively expensive for already weak institutions. This observation reinforces the argument that the gradations in risk-adjustment should be introduced slowly, so that institutions can adapt their behavior over time by improving their management control practices in addition to reducing their risk exposure and thus the subsidy they are to receive from their stronger peers.

Given the difficulty in executing an equitable system of risk-adjusting premiums, a surprisingly large number of countries attempt to do so. The systems in 24 countries (Argentina, Canada, Colombia, Ecuador, El Salvador, Finland, France, Germany's private system, Hungary, Italy, Kazakhstan, Macedonia, Mexico, Norway, Peru, Poland, Portugal, Romania, Sweden, Taiwan Province of China, Turkey, the United States, and its two Asian island protectorates—the Marshall Islands and Micronesia) currently set risk-adjusted insurance premiums (column 6, Table A4).[63] This is a marked increase in number from earlier in the decade of the 1990s.

Deposit Coverage

Limiting the coverage offered by the system of deposit insurance is the most common way to contain the moral hazard that deposit protection offers both to banks and their depositors. The actual objectives chosen for the system will influence a number of decisions that have to be made. These decisions include: (1) what types of institutions should be eligible to join the system; (2) which financial instruments should be covered; (3) which types of depositors should be covered and which excluded; (4) the amount that is covered; (5) whether the basic amount should be covered in full or whether a haircut should be imposed on the covered amount under a system of coinsurance; and (6) deciding whether to switch to full coverage in a systemic emergency. This survey examines country practices with regard to all of the seven questions.

While country objectives were not explicitly surveyed, clearly they will influence membership and coverage. It is, for example, possible to discern from countries' behavior with regard to coverage that in most countries, consumer protection is one of the top priorities for a system. Deposit insurance is designed to conserve the time and money of the small depositor for whom it is not feasible or not cost-effective to

monitor the condition of his/her bank. Protecting the stability of the financial system by promoting confidence and avoiding bank runs is a second high-priority objective. Resolution of a number of conceptual and practical issues follow from a careful explication of the system's priorities.

Limited and Full Coverage

Currently, almost all countries place limits on the explicit coverage they offer. Six countries (Ecuador, Honduras, Japan, Korea, Mexico, and Turkey) that normally have explicit but limited coverage, have temporarily, but explicitly, extended full coverage during times of acute financial distress (see Table A5 of the Statistical Appendix).[64] These countries plan to return to limited coverage when they can. An additional three countries without a system of deposit insurance (Indonesia, Malaysia, and Thailand) have explicitly extended full coverage during their financial emergencies, and all but Malaysia have already announced their intention to convert to limited coverage when their crises are over.

Setting the Limits on Coverage

The coverage limit should be low enough to encourage large depositors and sophisticated creditors to monitor and discipline their bank. Sophisticated depositors exert this discipline by demanding higher deposit rates from weaker banks in compensation for the higher risk of loss they are accepting; in other circumstances, depositors may withhold funds entirely from a particularly troubled bank.

There is a wide range to the limits that a country sets for its deposit insurance system, but there is greater uniformity in the European Union, where a minimum coverage (€20,000 in the year 2000) is prescribed. Translating the limits countries offer into either 1998 dollars or euros, coverage ranges from the dollar equivalent of a low of $120 in Ukraine to a high of $253,520 in Norway (excluding countries offering a full guarantee). While Germany's official scheme offers limited coverage, Beck (2000) argues that the private system offers virtually unlimited coverage to customers of member commercial banks. Corrective discipline is exercised by fellow members, which will be assessed ex post to meet deficiencies, rather than by depositors.

Any given limit expressed in dollar values (as in column 2 of Table A5) will be more generous in a country that has a low level of per capita income than where incomes are higher. While IMF staff typically uses the world average of per capita GDP as a

---

[63]Each of these systems is compulsory despite the risk-adjusted premiums.

[64]Jamaica recently ended its full coverage.

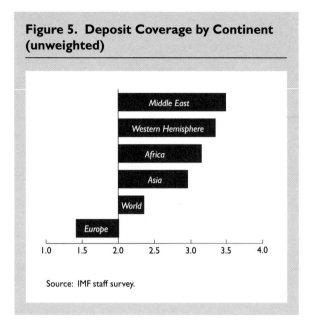

Figure 5. Deposit Coverage by Continent (unweighted)

Source: IMF staff survey.

limit. Consequently, Figure 1 shows coverage per capita country by country and Figure 5 shows that the unweighted average coverage ratio worldwide is 2.4 times per capita GDP; with the highest average in the Middle East and the lowest in Europe. The weighted average is lower at 2.1 times per capita GDP. This number falls to 1.8 times per capita GDP if the largest country, the United States, which has relative high coverage, is excluded. The individual country offering the highest per capita coverage is Oman, which guaranteed up to 8.8 times 1999 per capita GDP. The lowest ratio for coverage that appears in the survey is that of Ukraine, which covers only a small fraction of per capita GDP.

As Figure 6 shows, countries typically cover a high percentage of the number of deposit accounts. Excluding countries offering a comprehensive guarantee, the percentage of accounts covered in full is typically over 90 percent, although it is lower in Kenya, Nigeria, Sri Lanka, and Tanzania (see Table A6 of the Statistical Appendix). As is appropriate, the guarantee covers a typically much smaller percentage of the value of deposits, ranging from negligible in Estonia and Sri Lanka, to 12 percent in Tanzania, to a high of 76 percent in Norway (see Figure 7).

rough rule of thumb for appropriately limiting coverage, coverage observed in the survey is sometimes high and can considerably exceed the rule-of-thumb

Figure 6. Percentage of the Number of Depositors Covered

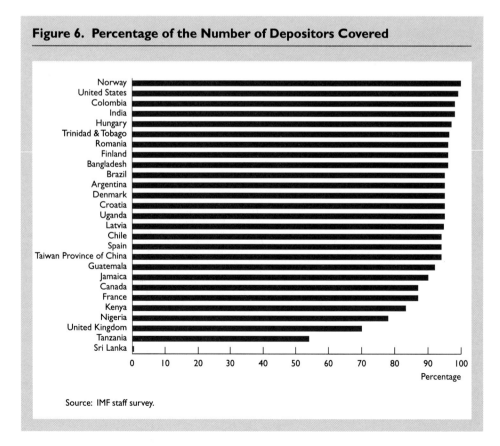

Source: IMF staff survey.

Figure 7. Percentage of the Value of Deposits Covered

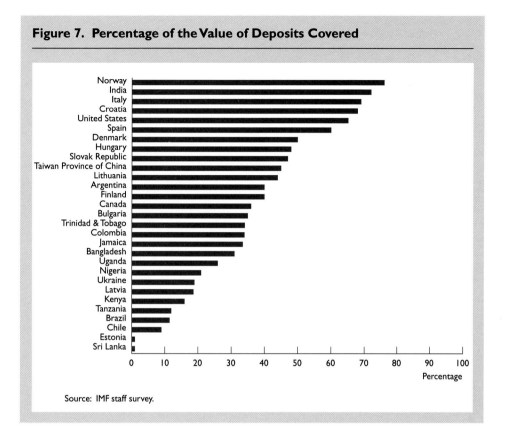

Source: IMF staff survey.

Adjusting the Limits on Coverage

Coverage can be adjusted upwards over time to reflect higher GDP and faster rates of inflation. If the coverage ratio was initially set very low because the system fund needed time to build its resources, the level can be raised as the fund matures. The adjustments can be made by indexing coverage or making, preferably rare, adjustments. There is both an advantage and a disadvantage to indexing coverage levels. The advantage is that it avoids setting unduly high limits initially; the disadvantage is that it will be hard for the public to keep abreast of repeated changes in the coverage level. Also, indexing coverage typically results in unrounded numbers, whereas round figures are easier to remember and use.

Applying the Limit Per Deposit or Per Depositor

Conceptually, a country could apply its coverage limit to each and every deposit that a depositor held anywhere in the country. This would allow a depositor to split his/her funds into a number of accounts at the same bank and gain virtually unlimited coverage. Far fewer countries do this today than did a few years ago. There has been a shift from per-deposit to per-depositor coverage since the earlier surveys

(Kyei 1995; Lindgren and Garcia 1996). In fact, per-deposit coverage is offered in only one country (the Dominican Republic) today.

Most countries apply their limit to the sum of all the deposits that a customer holds at any particular bank. This arrangement allows a depositor to obtain coverage above the limit by splitting his/her funds across a number of banks. This relaxes the limit somewhat, but does not allow the largest depositors to obtain full coverage. Some countries might want to go further and seek to limit coverage at any point in time to the sum of any individual depositor's accounts across all banks, regardless of the number of accounts held in any or all banks. In fact, Chile attempts to do this by imposing a limit on coverage available in any year on deposits held by any single depositor anywhere in the financial system.

Coinsurance

Some countries attempt to strike a balance between discouraging moral hazard and avoiding systemic runs by adopting a system of coinsurance. In 20 deposit insurance systems (those in Austria, Bahrain, Bulgaria, Chile, Colombia, the Czech Republic, the Dominican Republic, Estonia, Germany, Gibraltar, Ireland, Italy, Kazakhstan, Lithuania, Luxembourg, Macedonia, Oman, Poland, Portugal, and the United Kingdom) the depositor loses a small percentage of the covered deposit but is reimbursed for the majority by the system. (See column 5 of Table A5). The haircut commonly ranges from 10 percent to 25 percent, but some countries, such as Bulgaria and Kazakhstan, have multiple tranches on which they impose successively higher haircuts that range up to 50 percent of the initial deposit. To protect "widows and orphans," it is preferable to cover a very small deposit in full and coinsure above that level. This dual arrangement will reduce the incentive for retail runs while maintaining market discipline. In fact, 15 countries impose a haircut on all of the insured deposit, while only five use coinsurance above the basic coverage limit.

Which Deposits to Cover and Which to Exclude?

Most countries aim to protect small depositors while requiring larger depositors to monitor the condition of their bank and contain moral hazard. Of the two contrasting approaches used to achieve these two objectives, one makes the objective of deposit protection politically and conceptually clear, while the other is easier to administer and effect speedy compensation.[65]

The survey revealed that eight systems cover deposits of all types and 21 cover most kinds (see column 2 of Table A6). However, 17 systems exclude all foreign currency deposits and nine schemes in countries that are in, or aspire to be in, the European Union exclude some non-EU currency deposits from coverage. Some countries that cover foreign deposits (for example, France, Honduras, Jamaica, Latvia, and Ukraine, among others), pay out in domestic currency to help protect the system from exposure to foreign exchange risk. Fifty-four systems do not cover interbank deposits. Thirty-three systems exclude government deposits and 34 countries explicitly do not guarantee the deposits of insiders who could use privileged information to take advantage of the guarantee. Twenty-three countries explicitly exclude illegal deposits in their deposit insurance laws. Nine countries exclude deposits that pay exceptionally high rates. This exclusion serves to discourage weak institutions from bidding for deposits and gambling for recovery with the proceeds and

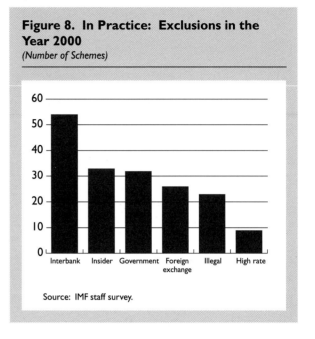

Figure 8. In Practice: Exclusions in the Year 2000
(Number of Schemes)

Source: IMF staff survey.

raising the costs of intermediation for their stronger competitors. Eighteen countries guarantee only, or mainly, household deposits. Evidently, as shown in Figure 8, a large number of countries find it worthwhile to undertake the administrative burden of giving preference to less sophisticated depositors—probably for political rather than financial reasons.

Full Coverage in a Crisis

Ecuador, Honduras, Japan, Indonesia, Korea, Malaysia, Mexico, Thailand, and Turkey currently offer coverage in full to depositors and creditors of all types and also most other liabilities. Chile covers demand deposits in full to protect the payment system, but offers limited coverage on other types of accounts. The comprehensive coverage in six of these countries (Ecuador, Honduras, Japan, Korea, Mexico, and Turkey) overrides the regular deposit insurance coverage in these countries. The other three countries previously had no explicit system.

Most of these countries began offering full coverage when they perceived a financial emergency, with the intention of replacing full emergency coverage with a limited system after the banking system had been restructured to soundness. Sweden, Finland, and Jamaica also offered full coverage during their financial crises but have already retracted it and replaced it with a system of limited coverage. As discussed further in Section IV, Indonesia, Malaysia, Thailand, and Turkey plan to replace their comprehensive guarantees when their crises are over, but have not specified a time for doing so. Ecuador plans to limit coverage

---

[65]The U.S. Federal Deposit Insurance Corporation (FDIC) and the Canada Deposit Insurance Corporation (CDIC) each have computer programs into which they feed a failed institution's data to identify insured depositors and the amounts owed to them. The fewer the exclusions from coverage, the more effective are these programs. Lacking exclusions, the FDIC typically compensates depositors within three days.

in the year 2001, Japan and Honduras in 2002, Korea by the end of 2000, and Mexico plans to complete phasing out its blanket coverage by 2005.

Timing the Repayment

The speed with which a depositor regains access to his funds affects the value of the coverage offered. Delay reduces any stated coverage value according to the time-value of money and the inconvenience imposed on the depositor by the delay. Whatever the degree of coverage, small depositors at failed banks typically need access to their insured funds rapidly. In effect, delaying payment reduces the value of coverage and increases systemic uncertainty. Thus, it behooves the deposit insurer to compensate insured depositors immediately, but certainly within 30 days; otherwise, the credibility of the system can be undermined, depositors may run from weak banks, and the retail payment systems may be disrupted. Depositors, finding themselves without their transactions and savings balances, may curtail their expenditure, which can cause or exacerbate a recession. The FDIC's practice of paying compensation within three days is a good example of prompt payment. In many countries, however, the survey found that repayment is remarkably slow. The EU Directive allows countries three months to make payment, but allows them to extend the time period in unusual circumstances. (Column 4, Table A7.)

Governance

Correct alignment of the deposit protection scheme with respect to three topics facilitates control over agency problems.[66] The first necessity is to ensure adequate funding. The second is to specify clearly the system's role and responsibilities. They were discussed earlier. The third is to design an appropriate organizational structure.

Organizational Structure

In the quest for potential independence and appropriate accountability, in 29 countries the deposit insurer constitutes a separate, independent legal entity (see column 6 of Table A8). Nevertheless, in a number of instances, it was, either in law or in practice, under the control of a government agency, which is usually the central bank or the ministry of finance,

but is sometimes the bank supervisor. The deposit insurer was found to be subordinate to the central bank in one-third of the countries, and to either the ministry of finance or the supervisory agency in another third. Even so, the deposit insurance agency does not normally have the power to grant or withdraw bank licenses, to supervise, or to provide lender-of-last-resort credit to failing banks, because that would detract from the stature of the supervisor and possibly diminish its effectiveness.

The Board of Directors

The survey shows that privately run systems are operated by bankers, who also typically are included on the boards of jointly run systems, while less frequently on government-run systems (see column 6, Table A8). Government-run schemes typically include representatives of the supervisory agency, the ministry of finance, and the central bank represented *ex officio* on the board of the deposit insurance agency. In relatively few instances, the chairman and the majority of the board are worthy, experienced, but independent members of the public with no current ties to the banking industry.

Good practices suggest that the government should provide back-up funding. Consequently, leaving financial decisions to a board of bankers is likely to result in an underfunded scheme. Nevertheless, the privately run schemes in Argentina and Germany have been successful to date. However, bankers can form a consultative committee to advise the board of a publicly funded deposit insurance scheme. There is a wide dispersion in arrangements regarding the running of the system. Thirteen schemes are privately administered, 39 are run by the government, and 16 are jointly operated (columns 3–5, Table A8). The authorities are able to exert some influence over some privately run schemes, such as those in Argentina and Brazil.

The danger of banks providing insufficient private resources to maintain the solvency of the fund, as they hope to be subsidized by a government, appears to be a reality in more than half of the systems surveyed. Nine of the privately run systems and 12 of the 16 jointly run systems have financial backing from the government. The remaining privately run schemes and 4 jointly operated systems, however, have attempted to avoid this particular agency problem by refraining from providing government financial support. In some cases, the law is silent on the subject of funding; in others, government financial backing is explicitly foresworn. However, whether those governments that have made a precommitment not to fund the system can sustain this commitment in face of an underfunded system remains to be seen.

---

[66]As discussed in footnote 1, agency problems involve a lack of coincidence between the principal in a transaction and the party acting as the agent for its execution.

Table 3. Characteristics of Deposit Insurance Systems by Continent in 1995 and 2000

	Number of Deposit Insurance Systems			Is Compulsory		Has Mainly a Fund		Risk-Adjusts Premiums		Administration						Coverage					
										Private		Joint		Government		Household		No interbank		No forex	
	1995	2000	% Growth	1995	2000	1995	2000	1995	2000	1995	2000	1995	2000	1995	2000	1995	2000	1995	2000	1995	2000
Africa	4	4	0	4	4	4	4	0	0	0	1	0	0	4	3	1	0	3	2	3	3
Asia	7	10	43	4	7	7	10	2	4	1	0	2	1	4	9	0	2	5	7	3	5
Europe	23	32	39	11	31	13	25	0	12	7	10	5	11	7	12	5	12	11	31	4	12
Middle East	2	4	100	1	4	1	3	0	0	1	0	0	2	0	2	0	0	0	2	0	1
Americas	11	17	55	6	16	9	16	2	8	0	2	4	2	6	13	0	4	2	12	1	5
Total	47	67	43	26	62	34	58	4	24	9	13	11	16	21	39	6	18	21	54	11	26

Source: IMF staff survey.

Trends and Convergence to Good Practice

A number of major changes in deposit insurance practices can be observed in comparison to the earlier surveys of Kyei (1995) and Lindgren and Garcia (1996). A summary comparison between the present survey and that of Kyei (1995) is presented in Table 3. It shows that there are many more (67) explicit systems in 2000 than there were in 1995, since a number of the countries listed in Kyei (1995) as having implicit schemes have replaced them with formal, explicit schemes in a major shift toward following good practices. In addition, other countries that were not included in the survey by Kyei have also recently put in place explicit systems.

A number of other trends have developed since Kyei's survey. First, the increase in formal systems has been marked in Europe, where the number has risen from 23 in 1995 to 32 in 1999. There has been no increase in the number (4) of systems in Africa, although six Central African countries agreed to form a regional system of deposit insurance in 1999. A year later, however, only two of the signatories have ratified the agreement, which will not go into effect until all do so. There has also been some growth in the number of systems in the Middle East and the Americas. In the Western Hemisphere, the number of explicit systems has risen to 17 in 2000 from 11 in 1995. In addition, a number of additional countries in the Americas are planning to introduce formal systems to replace their implicit ones. The introduction of new systems may be expected in Asia as countries recover from their financial crises and replace the full guarantees they have put in place with limited coverage.

Second, more countries—more than one-third of the total—now risk-adjust their deposit insurance premiums. Only two countries (other than the United States' protectorates in Asia) were identified in Kyei (1995) as adjusting their insurance premiums for risk. The increase in risk-adjusting countries has occurred in Africa, Europe, and the Americas. Assuming that the risk-adjustment is being well executed, this change constitutes a substantial shift toward good practices.

Third, there is a shift away from voluntary systems to compulsory schemes. Today, nine of every ten systems seek to avoid adverse selection in this way, whereas only just over half did so in the mid-1990s. The switch has occurred not only in Europe, as a result of the 1994 European Union Directive on Deposit Guarantee Schemes, but the trend has also been noticeable in the Middle East and in the Americas.[67]

Fourth, there has also been a trend toward funded systems. While only a few countries have switched from ex post levies to funded systems, newly created systems have almost universally been funded. (Gibraltar's new scheme is the exception in that it follows the ex post practice of the United Kingdom.) Funded schemes are universal in Africa and Asia and have increased elsewhere to reach dominance worldwide. Schemes that maintain a fund have been observed above to be more rule-based and less ambiguous in practice than the ex post systems favored by bankers' clubs. In this respect, the recent emphasis on funded systems is another example of convergence toward good practices.

---

[67]While the regional scheme agreed to in Africa in 1999 would be voluntary, the signatories attempted to combat adverse selection by proposing to risk adjust premiums.

Fifth, while most systems continue to be funded primarily by their member institutions, an increasing proportion of systems have access to back-up funding from the government, as recommended in Section II. In 2000, over three-quarters of systems have received or can expect to receive government assistance when necessary. There has been a small commensurate shift—from just under to slightly more than half—in favor of public administration of systems. This shift is to be expected as government funding is likely to be accompanied by government control. The remaining systems of deposit insurance divide themselves between privately run and jointly run schemes.

Sixth, virtually all countries now provide coverage per depositor, rather than per deposit, which tends to lower the effective coverage ratio. The reduction in the number of per-deposit coverage noted in 1996 survey has continued so that by 2000, the number had been reduced further to only one country.

There is also an increasing standardization of practices with regard to system coverage as a result of a EU directive, particularly among those countries that are, or aspire to be, members of the European Union. In the interests of competitive equity among banks from different countries, the EU directive diverges from good practice in one respect, however. By requiring the same minimum coverage limit (€20,000 by year 2000) in all member countries, the directive provides low per capita coverage in rich countries but a higher ratio in poorer countries within the European Union, which might, as a result, be more exposed to moral hazard.[68] However, the mandatory coverage is so low in rich countries that it remains relatively low even in less affluent EU countries, so that moral hazard from this source is unlikely to be a serious problem. Because there is so little variation in coverage, the correlation coefficient between per capita GDP and the coverage ratio is not significantly different from zero among member countries of the European Union, suggesting that

moral hazard is not a problem there. Nevertheless, it could be a problem for countries outside the European Union that aspire to join the Union and so emulate the European Union's deposit insurance system coverage even when it is many times their per capita GDP.

Worldwide, there is a small but statistically significant negative relationship between per capita GDP and the deposit insurance coverage ratio. That is, poorer countries, on average, offer higher coverage in relation to GDP than do richer countries. Perhaps they do so to enable their banks to complete internationally and to discourage deposits from migrating abroad. The inverse relationship is evident in all regions except Europe, but is particularly strong in Africa. This result indicates that moral hazard is present worldwide, but is stronger in developing countries than in Europe.

Despite shifts in favor of good practice, areas remain for improvement. For example, some countries have not resolved the potential conflict of having a privately run system of deposit insurance with government financial support. In addition, deposit compensation practices are often surprisingly slow. This problem may be exacerbated by an increasing trend toward excluding categories of depositors from coverage. For example, a large increase in the restriction of system protection to individuals, households, and nonprofit organizations is observable, mostly because former Soviet countries made explicit their old practice of guaranteeing household deposits. Such restrictions have been adopted by over one-quarter of countries, whereas only one-eighth did so in 1995. There has also been an increase (from 45 percent to 80 percent) in the number of systems that exclude interbank deposits from coverage. The change occurred in both Europe, where the EU Directive on Deposit Guarantee Schemes lists interbank deposits as a candidate for exclusion, and also in the Americas. There has also been, perhaps surprisingly in light of the recent currency crises, a trend—apparent on all continents—toward excluding foreign currency deposits from coverage. In 2000, 39 percent of countries excluded all or some deposits denominated in foreign currency.

---

[68]€20,000 is 0.4 times per capita GDP in Luxembourg, which had the highest per capita GDP in the European Union in 1998, but more than twice per capita GDP in Portugal.

IV   On Instituting and Removing a Full "Blanket" Guarantee

While a well-designed, limited system of deposit insurance can protect small depositors' funds in normal times, help to avoid unjustified runs, and provide a framework for the efficient resolution of individual failed banks—thus enhancing systemic stability—a limited system cannot be expected to maintain systemic stability in the face of an unforeseen shock of massive proportions or where weaknesses have been allowed to become so widespread that the system shudders even in response to smaller shocks. Faced with such a scenario and recognizing that financial stability is a public good, the government may decide to take emergency action to preserve the stability of the financial sector. It may also choose to bear the costs of the economic emergency and override the system of limited deposit protection and offer a full, temporary guarantee of depositors and creditors to ensure the continued functioning of the financial system. That guarantee should, however, be removed as soon as possible and replaced by a formal, limited, compulsory system of deposit protection that is funded by the banking system and supported by a good incentive structure, including effective regulation and supervision.

Indications of Systemic Instability

A systemic crisis can be defined in a number of ways. However, following Sundararajan and Baliño (1991) and Lindgren, Garcia, and Saal (1996), the phrase is used after the event to refer to cases where there are "runs or other substantial portfolio shifts, collapses of financial firms, or massive government intervention."[69] Ex ante, identifying a system crisis is more difficult.

There are, in fact, a number of indications of problems that are so severe that they cause the government to consider instituting a full guarantee. The typical developing-crisis scenario is one in which insolvencies begin to be perceived by the markets. The crisis will become transparent when liquidity prob-

lems occur in individual banks, there is segmentation and eventual non-acceptance in the interbank market(s), customers (both depositors and creditors) withdraw significant amounts of their funds or refuse to renew their contracts, banks engage in distress bidding for deposits,[70] the market becomes aware of shortfalls under reserve requirements, and/or banks incur overdrafts at the central bank. Such problems indicate that the system is deteriorating beyond the capacity of the banks to handle their difficulties by themselves and are indicative of an incipient, possibly systemic, crisis that will destroy confidence in the financial system. These problems typically become evident in the operation of the payment system, where risks of disruptions and payment defaults become pervasive. These indications of banks' insurmountable problems typically become apparent first to large and informed creditors, who tend to run first.

Identifying (in advance) what problem should be regarded as systemic will depend not just on the proportion of banks or bank assets that are in trouble but also on country-specific factors. These factors include, among others, the structure of the financial system, the macroeconomic environment, the state of public confidence in the financial system, and the ability of the authorities to finance and commit to a restoration strategy. As observed in a number of countries, it is not always possible to agree on whether or not a crisis is, or, even after the event, was systemic. It is a judgment call.

Should a Deposit Insurance System Be Introduced in a Time of Crisis?

Should a limited system of deposit insurance be introduced when a country perceives the signs of crisis described above? Or when it fears for other reasons that it might experience a banking crisis? The author-

---

[69]See Lindgren, Garcia, and Saal (1996, page 20).

[70]Distress bidding for deposits occurs where a problem bank that would become illiquid bids up deposit rates in order to attract funds.

ities have considered doing so in many countries, but, as explained above, deposit insurance is no substitute for government support in a systemic crisis. IMF staff advice, therefore, has been not to introduce a limited deposit insurance scheme until the banking system or its major banks have been restructured to acceptable financial soundness that is judged mainly in terms of their solvency and profitability.

Losses are realized when banks fail. To the extent possible, the government should seek to share these losses with owners, depositors, and creditors. Doing so will reduce government outlays and keep moral hazard in check. A limited deposit insurance system facilitates the loss distribution process. However, in cases where the condition of a large portion of the banking system is in doubt and may require large payments from the system, the system will often fall short of resources even if a substantial fund has been accumulated.[71] In some instances, the system's losses will be too large to be absorbed by the banking system even over an extended period of time. While it is true that a system that gives itself or depositors, especially small ones, priority over the assets of a failed bank helps to reduce demands on the insurance scheme, this will not protect it from bankruptcy when bank losses are severe.

Many countries have chosen to provide officially limited, but generous, deposit guarantees, especially in times of crisis. It would have been preferable if they had taken early action to strengthen their banking systems. But some have not done so, so that by the time problems erupt, they believe they must initiate extensive, even comprehensive, deposit guarantees to maintain confidence. Once a generous or full guarantee has been provided, however, it is typically difficult to reduce the coverage to restore market discipline to the financial system. Consequently, countries tend to retain the guarantee and seek to rely excessively on formal systems of regulation and supervision and on other restrictive measures to alleviate the contrary incentives that an excessive guarantee provides. They are, however, unlikely to be successful in strengthening their banking system through supervision alone, especially if systemic bank restructuring has not been undertaken.

Allocating the Losses Caused by Bank Failures

In this situation, the government has a choice—either to absorb the losses itself or to allocate those that have already occurred among the parties involved. (The bank's owners stand first in line to absorb losses. The holders of subordinated debt are second.) Countries could, but have not explicitly written down banks' debts. Instead, some have frozen deposits temporarily, reduced the rates paid on deposits, relied on inflation to cut real values, converted private sector claims on banks into long-term bonds or equity, or imposed a special levy on social banks.[72]

Imposing Special Levies

Before it institutes a full guarantee, a deposit insurer may impose special charges on sound banks. These special charges exceed the regular system premiums in order to compensate the system for the losses incurred by weak banks that it has covered. Special charges, which can extend over a number of years, can be justified, since all banks, including sound banks, benefit from the overall stability in the banking system and from the orderly exit of failed banks. In fact, a deposit insurance fund can itself be regarded as a formalized instrument for all banks to share in funding the losses of weak banks. This loss sharing should not, of course, be allowed to jeopardize the viability of surviving banks.

Should a Full Guarantee Be Provided?

In normal circumstances, the cost of dealing with individual bank failures falls first on the owners and subordinated debt holders, and then on the large depositors, creditors, and the deposit insurance system. Deposit insurance cannot be expected to deal with widespread insolvencies arising from external shocks, major macroeconomic imbalances, or accumulated microeconomic mismanagement. Imposing very extensive special charges on sound banks could destroy them, lead to financial instability and runs on other banks.

Thus, in case of a systemic crisis, the government's objectives for depositor protection change. There is then a need to protect the payment system and avoid depositors' "flight to quality," which may involve a flight to cash, other banks, or abroad. In such a situation, the government needs to take control, declare a "state of economic emergency" and possibly establish a temporary resolution authority to deal with the crisis in order to restore confidence and provide a breathing space to make necessary re-

---

[71]The best example of this is the United States where, even after 50 years of accumulating funds, widespread failures of savings and loan associations (S&Ls) bankrupted the S&L insurance fund.

[72]Converting deposits to equity will assist solvency. Converting short-term deposits to a longer term will help liquidity, but not solvency, unless the nominal value of deposits is also written down. See Baer and Klingebiel (1995) for examples of countries that have adopted these techniques.

forms. Thus, dealing with a systemic crisis calls for actions that reach beyond the system of limited deposit insurance. In a systemic crisis, a full guarantee can be helpful, even essential.[73] That opinion has been strengthened by experiences gained during the recent crises in Asia and other countries. For a guarantee to be credible, it must be tailored to recognize fiscal realities. A guarantee by a nearly insolvent government may not be credible and therefore may be meaningless.

Making the Decision

A government has a number of decisions to make when it is faced with a financial crisis. If the government judges the crisis *not* to be systemic, it will typically use its usual methods of resolving bank weaknesses and failures. If it judges the crisis to be systemic or nearly systemic, it has to consider offering a comprehensive guarantee.

To prevent or control a crisis, the government may decide to extend explicit blanket guarantees to all depositors and also to creditors to maintain confidence in banks and thus prevent a run on banks or the banking system, avoid capital outflows, and aid the economy to recover from the financial shock by ensuring the continuing supply of banking and payment services. This was done in Finland and Sweden in 1992, by Japan and Mexico in 1995,[74] by Indonesia, Korea, Malaysia, and Thailand during the Asian crises,[75] and also by Jamaica in 1997, Kuwait implicitly in 1992, and Turkey in 1999.

Not all countries that have faced a systemic crisis have granted a comprehensive guarantee, how-

Table 4. Response to Selected Systemic Crises

Countries That Gave a Full Guarantee	Countries That Did Not Give a Full Guarantee
Ecuador	Bulgaria
Finland	Czech Republic
Honduras[1]	Estonia
Indonesia	Latvia
Jamaica	Lithuania
Japan	Mongolia
Korea	Norway[2]
Kuwait	Philippines
Malaysia	Poland
Mexico	Romania
Sweden	Russia
Thailand	
Turkey	

Source: IMF staff survey.

[1]Honduras provides government bonds when a deposit exceeds the insurance limit and the assets of the failed bank.

[2]A generous guarantee was given by the Government Bank Insurance Fund. There was not a full guarantee by the government per se.

ever.[76] As shown in Table 4, for example, a number of countries, many in Eastern Europe and the Commonwealth of Independent States did not place a full guarantee when their banking systems experienced systemic problems. This was partly due to a lack of fiscal capacity and partly because depositors were concentrated in the large state-owned savings bank. The government was concerned that a full guarantee would allow insolvent and illiquid banks to bid deposits away from the state bank.

Weighing the Costs and Benefits

The direct and indirect costs of supporting the guarantee can be substantial, but the losses from not doing so can be greater. The guarantee requires providing liquidity to banks to allow depositors and creditors to withdraw their funds at will. The introduction of a comprehensive guarantee should include a conscious decision that the value of maintaining a payment system and the supply of credit exceed costs

---

[73]See Folkerts-Landau, Lindgren, and others (1998, pp. 28–30). But in crisis situations, including those that disrupt the payment system, the government will need to take some of the financial responsibility and do what it should have done before—strengthen the financial system so that it will be more able to withstand shocks and not propagate or spread them. This strengthening should include preparing concomitant reforms to minimize immediate losses in the payment system, and eliminate future losses in the banking system.

[74]Argentina did not issue an explicit guarantee although the banking system's deposits declined by 18 percent in the early months of 1995. Some depositors lost money at this time and a few small banks were closed. Nevertheless, beginning in March 1995, the authorities implicitly extended a 100 percent guarantee to bank deposits, while avoiding formal violation of the currency board arrangement. It did so by the central bank providing all the liquidity that banks suffering withdrawals needed, so that any depositor who wished to do so could withdraw his deposits, thus fully protecting depositors. The central bank provided liquidity by reducing reserve requirements across the board and by granting rediscounts to the largest state-owned bank, which, in turn, provided liquidity to the rest of the system.

[75]Sweden, Finland, and Jamaica have already scaled down their coverage to that more typical of a limited deposit insurance guarantee, and the other crisis countries are preparing to do so.

[76]Depositors and/or creditors incurred losses in Argentina in 1989–90, Brazil in 1994–96, Chile in 1982–84, Côte d'Ivoire in 1991, Estonia in 1992, Latvia in 1995, Malaysia in 1986–88, Thailand in 1983–87 and in 1997, and the United States since 1991. See "Systemic Bank Restructuring and Macroeconomic Policy" (Table 2). Moreover, depositors at some, but not all failed banks, incurred losses in the Venezuelan crisis of 1994–95.

of providing the guarantee. Opponents of granting a decree will be concerned about creating moral hazard and meeting the potentially large cost of compensating those who are guaranteed. However, a guarantee is most cost effective if it is not used, which requires that the promised coverage be credible. The government or agency that issues the guarantee will need to have explicit legal backing and fiscal resources for the promise to be believable.

The blanket guarantee may have benefits. The losses of banks and the economy in general may be lower, confidence should be greater, both the payment and the financial system should function more efficiently, and the authorities' responses to the crises should be improved by the greater time available for making good decisions.

A guarantee may be implemented to promote confidence in the financial sector; stabilize the liabilities of guaranteed institutions; gain time to organize and execute systemic bank restructuring; and preserve the integrity of the payment system. A full guarantee may be a necessary condition for containing a financial crisis, but it is not a sufficient one. It cannot restore confidence in a currency crisis or prevent the capital flight that occurs when a country experiences economic or political turmoil, but it can reduce their severity.

Principles to Follow When Offering a Full Guarantee

If it decides that the benefits of providing a blanket guarantee outweigh the costs, the government will provide full coverage. There are certain basic, general principles that it should then observe in granting comprehensive guarantees. For example, full guarantees should not be made a regular part of the financial landscape; otherwise such an action would increase moral hazard. Guarantees should be granted only in economic emergencies to calm the markets and give the government (some) time to study and implement its corrective policies. By not giving explicit guarantees ahead of an emergency, the government is left with flexibility to work out the particular solution that is most compatible with market incentives and the availability of fiscal resources. Sharing losses with creditors and large depositors and closing individual failed banks before the guarantee is given will prove least expensive in the long run.

Many of the good practices appropriate in normal times are also relevant during a systemic crisis (Table 5). There are several differences, however. The responsibility may or may not fall to the deposit insurance agency, but it should be clearly defined and publicly understood. The guarantee must be publicly provided to ensure the credibility needed to avoid its being used. Whereas limited coverage should be offered in perpetuity, full coverage must be temporary and must be known to be temporary, to limit moral hazard. This problem must be tackled also by strengthening supervision and regulation.

Credibility

Just as a limited system of deposit insurance will not sustain financial stability in a systemic crisis, for similar reasons, placing a full guarantee that exceeds the government's capacity to pay will not restore confidence in a crisis. Consequently, the guarantee that is given must be tailored to fit financial reality. The tailoring may involve excluding certain classes of institutions, certain financial instruments, or certain classes of creditors from coverage. Those excluded may incur losses.

To effect a credible guarantee, the authorities must then choose: (1) when and how to provide the guarantee; (2) which financial institutions to include; (3) which financial instruments to cover; (4) which types of depositors and creditors to protect; (5) in which currency to provide compensation; (6) how to deal with disruptions to the payment system; and (7) what measures to take to ameliorate the moral hazard that the guarantee carries.

How and When Should the Guarantee Be Provided?

The existence and provisions of the guarantee should be precisely specified in emergency legislation or decree, and the terms should authoritatively be made clear to the public. Judging the correct language and tone to use in making the public announcement of the guarantee is crucial to restoring public confidence. While the government may be able to share costs of bank failures at the beginning of a crisis, it foregoes the option to impose losses on creditors and depositors once it has put a full guarantee into effect. Consequently, judging the correct moment to enact and announce the decree is difficult but important for its effectiveness and cost. Placing it too quickly can weaken market discipline in the financial system, while waiting too long can destroy public confidence, which will be difficult to rebuild. Skill is required in judging the optimal timing for placing a full guarantee so that its validity is not called into question and it is not called upon to provide large amounts of compensation to those benefiting from a guarantee that is called or unnecessary comfort if it is not called.

Dealing With Deficiencies in the Infrastructure

The country will need to show that it intends to make progress toward legal, judicial, accounting, fi-

Table 5. Good Practices for Blanket Coverage in a Systemic Crisis

	Good Practice for Deposit Insurance Systems	Good Practices for Full Guarantees
Infrastructure	1. Have realistic objectives.	Have realistic objectives.
	2. Choose carefully between a public or private deposit insurance system.	Provide publicly a full guarantee.
	3. Define the deposit insurance agency's mandate accordingly.	Carefully assign and publicly announce the responsibility for effecting full guarantee. It may or may not be the deposit insurance agency's responsibility.
	4. Have a good legal, judicial, accounting, financial, and political infrastructure.	Have the same conditions, which remain essential.
Moral hazard	5. Define the system explicitly in law and regulation.	Adopt explicit systems; they are typically more effective than vague implicit guarantees.
	6. Give the supervisor a system of prompt remedial actions.	Ensure supervisor retains prompt corrective action.
	7. Resolve failed depository institutions promptly.	Resolve as promptly as is feasible.
	8. Provide low coverage permanently.	Provide full coverage temporarily.
	9. Net (offset) loans in default against deposits.	Offsetting past due loans is still appropriate.
Adverse selection	10. Make membership compulsory.	Blanket coverage is mandatory.
	11. Risk-adjust premiums, once the deposit insurance system has sufficient experience.	Risk adjusting remains appropriate where feasible.
Agency problems	12. Create an independent but accountable deposit insurance system agency.	Design an authority that is accountable and independent, to be in charge of resolving the crisis.
	13. Have bankers on an advisory board not dominating the main board of a deposit insurance system with access to government funding.	Not relevant.
	14. Ensure close relations with the lender of last resort and the supervisor.	Ensure that the agency in charge of implementing the full guarantee has close relations with the supervisor.
Financial integrity and credibility	15. Start when banks are sound.	Start only in a systemic crisis.
	16. Ensure adequate sources of funding (ex ante or ex post) to avoid insolvency.	Make sufficient funding available and ensure the public knows this.
	17. Invest fund resources wisely.	Not applicable.
	18. Pay out or transfer deposits quickly.	Provide liquidity to pay out deposits quickly.
	19. Ensure good information.	Ensure that those effecting the guarantee have good information to enable them to make wise decisions.
	20. Make appropriate disclosure.	Provide information to the public—it is essential for restoring confidence.

nancial and political reforms, if its temporary comprehensive guarantee is to be credible. Such reforms are likely to take place over a number of years.

What Should a Comprehensive Guarantee Cover?

Typically a full guarantee covers all bank debts to both depositors and other creditors. (As discussed above, protecting shareholders and subordinated debt holders is inappropriate unless they carry no responsibility for the plight of their banks). It must be decided whether the risks of exchange rate fluctuation and the inflation-induced erosion of real value will be covered.

Which Institutions Should Be Included in the Guarantee?

The authorities must decide which financial functions they seek to protect. Where commercial banks provide the principal means of intermediation and of collecting deposits, make loans, evaluate risks, facilitate the payment system, and transmit monetary policy to the economy, they would be the first candidates for inclusion in the guarantee. As the conjunction of deposit-taking and loan-granting makes institutions vulnerable to runs, other types of depository institutions, such as finance companies, merchant banks, savings banks, and credit unions could also be covered if they operate as near banks and play a sufficiently important role in the financial system and the economy.[77] In addition, institutions whose demise could contaminate the banking system should also be included. The composition of the set of guaranteed institutions will vary from country to country with local conditions. Domestic institutions and local subsidiaries, affiliates, and branches of foreign banks would typically be covered.[78]

When fiscal constraints are compelling, the government may decide to limit the institutions it will cover under the full guarantee to the core banking system in order to control its costs. It would be ill-advised to try to pre-specify which banks will emerge from the rehabilitation process that is to follow as the core banks in the system. To attempt to identify the core would require picking winners and losers in the race for survival, and the government's choice is likely to differ from the markets' determination. The core will emerge after the event. By not extending the guarantee to all banks, it needs to be assessed whether those that are not covered will fail; how extensive will be the losses that their creditors incur, and the social, political, and economic implications of these losses. Where compensation is offered, it must be speedy if it is to be credible; otherwise depositors will recognize that they are incurring losses in present value terms. A comprehensive guarantee in nearly all cases is basically a liquidity guarantee, so it must be satisfied on demand.

The decision on which types of institution to exclude would depend on where the government is prepared to impose losses and where it expects contagion to spread. To the extent that it fears runs and flight to quality at home and abroad by large creditors, the government will focus on guaranteeing the institutions that house the funds at risk of flight. To the extent that it is interested in protecting the smaller citizens from hardship caused by the financial crisis, it will also cover smaller, consumer-oriented institutions.

Which Creditors Should Be Protected?

The guarantee will be written in legal language to encompass those creditors whose flight could threaten the banking system. It will most probably protect both the domestic and foreign creditors of banks located onshore. Both large and small depositors and other creditors would be covered under the comprehensive guarantee.[79] Depositors and creditors of offshore centers would not be protected if the authorities want to send a message to sophisticated creditors in these locations that they are at risk. Offshore institutions often benefit from minimum regulation and lax supervision, so that investors should assess their exposure to loss accordingly. This will have to be judged case-by-case in view of the importance of the offshore center to the onshore sector. Some countries have chosen also to protect subordinated debt holders, while others, such as Indonesia, Korea, Malaysia, Mexico, and Thailand imposed losses on the holders of subordinated debt.[80]

Should External Creditors Be Protected?

The issues governing whether and how to cover external creditors are complex. Those countries that have offered guarantees to external creditors have done so in the hopes that the guarantees will increase the confidence of these creditors, who would be encouraged to roll over their loans and not add to the capital flight that may have already occurred. In many cases, however, external creditors have not rolled over their loans, and capital flight has continued.[81]

This observation raises important questions regarding whether, and to what extent, losses should be imposed on external creditors. This paper does not seek to answer this question, which remains to be resolved as one of the important issues regard-

---

[77]Korea, Malaysia, and Thailand, for example, included commercial banks, finance companies, and merchant banks in their guarantees (see Lindgren and others, 2000).

[78]Korea and Malaysia also included the overseas branches of domestic banking institutions in its guarantee. Some countries, such as Mexico and Korea, have extended coverage beyond depository institutions to insurance companies and brokerage houses, but not Korea's investment trust companies or leasing companies. Korea excluded repurchase agreements after July 1998, however, as a beginning to phasing out its full guarantee.

[79]In Indonesia, insider deposits were not covered by the guarantee (likewise in Thailand) unless claimants could prove that the transactions had been made at "arm's length."

[80]At least in the case of Thailand, losses can be imposed only when the bank is liquidated and not if it is intervened or reorganized with new shareholders.

[81]In Thailand, for example, foreign creditors rather than domestic depositors and creditors ran, even with a government guarantee in place. Sweden's full guarantee was, on the other hand, successful in stemming the flight of foreign capital. In Indonesia, both domestic depositors and foreign creditors ran. Korea negotiated a separate debt agreement with its foreign creditors that imposed losses on them. Evidently the guarantee was most credible in Sweden and least credible in Indonesia. A question arises regarding the reasons for these disparities in experience. Future research may determine the reasons for the differences in credibility.

ing private sector burden-sharing in the context of discussions on the new international financial architecture.

Which Instruments Should Be Encompassed in a Full Guarantee?

A country may formally guarantee only straightforward deposits, repurchase agreements, senior, and nonsubordinated debt instruments. In practice, it is virtually impossible to exclude derivatives and other off-balance-sheet contracts, once the institution ceases operations. This situation arises because derivatives often convert into the standard, on-balance-sheet instruments that would be covered by the comprehensive guarantee when one party to the contract defaults.

The Currency of Payment

Most countries that have offered a full guarantee on foreign currency liabilities have made payment in domestic currency valued at the current exchange rate. Korea, however, provided liquidity support to commercial banks in foreign currency.

Dealing with Disruptions to the Payment System

The agency responsible for the integrity of the payment system (often the central bank) can take several steps to reduce the risk of loss, alleviate the domino and contagion effects from the losses that do occur, and curtail the costs incurred by the deposit insurance system and the lender of last resort.

The central bank typically uses standing credit facilities, such as a Lombard facility, or intraday credit accommodation of payments to maintain liquidity in the payment system. Before the full guarantee is given, assisted by the supervisory authority, the central bank should ideally seek to accomplish the difficult task of distinguishing between illiquid and insolvent banks. It would lend to the illiquid but viable banks, and rely on the supervisor to deal firmly with nonviable banks. However, when problem banks are numerous, very large, or cannot be identified ex ante, it becomes difficult for the central bank to contain its lending for fear of triggering a systemic crisis. Before the full guarantee, central bank lending should be temporary, strictly limited, carry an explicit government guarantee,[82] and be considered as

the first step in a comprehensive financial and operational restructuring.[83]

Once the guarantee has been given, the central bank must provide the liquidity to honor it. That means providing liquidity first, before the bank's capital position is known. Capital deficiencies will be dealt with later by the deposit insurance system or in the budget. All concerned, however, need to clearly understand that the central bank has few real resources (capital and reserves) to deal with bank insolvencies, and that the government needs to stand behind all the credits that are extended by the central bank. To the extent that such credits are not repaid, their costs must be borne by the budget and, ultimately, by the taxpayer.

Concomitant Measures to Contain Moral Hazard

Countries have adopted a number of measures to control incentive problems. They include (1) in insolvent banks, writing down the owners' shares and subordinated debt-holders' claims and fully and replacing their management; (2) announcing that the full guarantee is only a temporary measure;[84] (3) capping the interest payable on deposits at some market determined rate;[85] (4) covering only the principal plus a limited amount of interest; (5) imposing a fee for the guarantee;[86] (6) intensifying the supervision of institutions encompassed under the comprehensive guarantee; (7) placing limits on asset growth in individual institutions; (8) ensuring that insiders and criminals are excluded; and (9) temporarily nationalizing banks that are recapitalized with public funds.

As discussed above, writing down the claims of shareholders and subordinated debt holders and replacing faulty management serves as a warning for such stakeholders to conduct their fiduciary steward-

---

[82]The guarantee would compensate the central bank for any resulting losses it incurs by reducing the central bank's remission of profits to the government or by providing additional capital, if necessary.

[83]Chile is the only country where the central bank provides a full guarantee for banks' demand deposits in addition to limited government coverage for household savings and time deposits. The quid pro quo for this guarantee is a 100 percent marginal reserve requirement on insured deposits when they exceed 250 percent of a bank's capital. Thus, this scheme reduces moral hazard by limiting banks' ability to acquire risky assets. At the margin, this arrangement approximates the concept of a narrow bank where all deposits are safely invested in government or other liquid securities.

[84]Indonesia, Japan, Korea, Mexico, and Thailand have announced that their full guarantee will be replaced by a limited system of deposit protection.

[85]Indonesia and Thailand capped rates at margins above those paid by the best banks to prevent aggressive bidding for deposits.

[86]Indonesia and Thailand imposed an additional fee for the comprehensive guarantee. Members of the deposit insurance system in Japan, Korea, and Mexico continue to pay premiums to their insurance fund while benefiting from the full guarantee.

ship responsibly in the future. Announcing that the full guarantee is temporary warns large depositors and creditors to keep monitoring the condition of their banks so that they can exert market discipline when the guarantee is removed. Capping interest rates and covering only principal plus limited interest both reduce the ability of weak banks to bid for deposits and to use the guaranteed funds so obtained to gamble for recovery or to loot the bank. These measures also reduce the financial obligation that the government must cover. Imposing a fee for the guarantee on all banks reduces adverse selection and helps to pay some of the government's costs of providing the guarantee. Intensifying supervision is necessary to prevent bank owners and managers from gambling for recovery, looting the bank, and from taking other actions that will weaken their bank.

A number, or all, of these measures are recommended as ways to reduce the much-feared moral hazard associated with granting full coverage. At the same time, moral hazard becomes less of an issue and is more easily managed when the crisis is fully transparent and the public recognizes that, temporarily, exceptional measures are necessary to contain it.

Finally, despite all efforts to follow good practices for installing a guarantee, the credibility of the guarantee will only be as good as the government's financial position. The government's solvency and liquidity, in turn, depend on the strength of the macroeconomic, microeconomic, and structural reforms undertaken to resolve the crisis.

On Removing a Global Guarantee

Global guarantees are typically provided in two conceptually different instances: in times of crisis for a wide range of financial institutions and in the normal course of events for state-owned banks. In both cases, these guarantees contain moral hazard, constitute major distortions, and should be phased out as soon as possible to improve the competitive efficiency of the banking system.

The Advisability of Removing Full Guarantees

The modalities of removing a full guarantee are currently of interest to a number of countries. Some countries have introduced a blanket guarantee for bank depositors and creditors during a crisis where there was no explicit deposit protection (as in Indonesia, Jamaica, Malaysia, Sweden, and Thailand) while others augmented the coverage offered by an existing system (as in Finland, Japan, Korea, and Mexico). Finland and Sweden subsequently have replaced their blanket guarantees with limited systems of deposit insurance; and Honduras, Indonesia, Ja-

maica, Japan, Mexico, Thailand, and Kuwait are preparing to do so.

A number of countries have given full guarantees to their state-owned banks. Some, including China and Costa Rica, are considering removing their full guarantees on state-owned banks. (Kuwait and China's guarantees are implicit, and Costa Rica's is explicit.)

Having the full guarantee in place is costly. It may involve explicit outlays and otherwise carry the costs inherent in a contingent liability, see Merton and Bodie, 1993. Whether it is called or not, it reduces market discipline and makes control exercised by supervisors the basic means for limiting perverse incentives. Thus, there is typically a need to scale down the guarantee once the crisis is over. To do so in a credible way normally requires new legislation to provide for the introduction of a limited deposit insurance system and an institutional infrastructure to support it (laws and regulations necessary for corrective actions and exit policies, and institution strengthening and supervision). This is the route that Finland and Sweden followed when they discontinued their emergency guarantees of all bank liabilities after their crises were resolved in the mid- to late 1990s and, at the same time, initiated a new or revised system of deposit insurance.

Following necessary restructuring of the banking system, improved macroeconomic policies, and measures to strengthen prudential regulation and supervision, an explicit, comprehensive guarantee should be replaced by a system of limited protection that is the same for large and small banks, whether they are state-owned or private. However, replacing a credible full guarantee with a limited system invites runs when the condition of the banks is weak or unknown. Thus good timing for removing the guarantee is essential.[87]

Timing the Removal

There is a trade-off with regard to timing the guarantee's removal. It is possible to retain the guarantee pending the dawn of the perfect day when every conceivably desirable condition has been met. But

---

[87]Not everyone favors replacing a full guarantee with limited deposit protection, however. Some argue that some countries have limited political capital available for dealing firmly with weak and failed banks and that what is available should be expended on isolating a small group of bank creditors (subordinated debt holders, in particular) as the only ones to stand at risk and monitor bank condition. Professor Charles Calomiris, for example, argues that, in practice, most creditors are protected, even in systems that have limited protection in place. Protection is effected by resolving failed banks by a purchase and assumption transaction that transfers all of a failed bank's debts to the acquiring bank. Thus, protection is limited in law, but not in practice. However, lessons learned from past crises are contesting Professor Calomiris' assertion of full protection.

Table 6. Length of Full Guarantees

Country	Date Placed	Date of/for Removal	Comments
Finland	February 2, 1993.	Removed on December 8, 1998.	The existing system of deposit insurance, in place before the full guarantee, was revised in 1998.
Honduras	September 1999.	September 2002.	Government bonds are issued to cover the amount of a deposit that exceeds both the limits of the insurance and the assets of the failed bank.
Jamaica	January 1997.	August 1998.	The full guarantee was removed when limited deposit insurance went into operation.
Japan	Announced June 1995, enacted into law in June 1996, and reiterated in November 1997.	To be removed in April 2002.	The authorities have delayed the removal of the full guarantee for one year until April 2002.
Korea	November 1997.	By December 2000.	The deposit insurance system, enacted in 1996 and overridden by the full guarantee, is to be revised.
Kuwait	1992.	No date has been set for cessation.	The guarantee is has been announced, but it is not written in law.
Malaysia	January 1998.	Not yet announced.	There has been some discussions concerning starting a system of deposit insurance to replace the blanket guarantee.
Mexico	Unclear.	To be phased out slowly by 2005.	The process of phasing out the full guarantee has already started.
Sweden	December 18, 1992.	Was removed on July 1, 1996.	Deposit insurance was started for the first time in 1996 to replace the full guarantee.
Thailand	September 1997.	Not yet announced.	The government is preparing a system of limited protection to replace the full guarantee.
Turkey	December 1999.	No date has been announced.	The guarantee has been announced but has not been written into the law.

Source: IMF staff survey.

that day may never come, so it may be preferable to remove the guarantee once a minimum set of conditions has been met. Some countries have adopted an intermediate course of action. They begin to phase out the full guarantee when they believe it will be a nonevent. The phasing out allows public confidence to be tested sequentially. More of the guarantee will be removed as more of the conditions for removal are met and the risk of runs has been reduced. A summary of country practices regarding the removal of blanket guarantees is given in Table 6.

The Ideal Time for Removal

To be certain to avoid disruption to the banking system, the partial guarantee would not be introduced ideally until (1) public confidence has been restored; (2) the banking system has been restructured successfully; (3) the crisis has passed; (4) the economy has begun to recover; (5) the macroeconomic environment is supportive of bank soundness; (6) the authorities possess, and are ready to use, strong remedial

and exit policies for banks that in the future are perceived by the public to be unsound; (7) appropriate accounting, disclosure, and legal systems are in place; (8) a strong prudential regulatory and supervisory framework is in operation; and (9) the public has been given adequate notice of the pending change.

These ideal conditions may never be met and there is a danger that the government will prolong the guarantee indefinitely, especially as a number of the conditions will take time to implement. The government must use its judgment that the immediate issues have been addressed and sufficient progress is being made toward achieving the longer term goals. In other words, the guarantee can be safely removed when it is no longer needed and removal is a "nonevent."[88]

---

[88]Professor Edward Kane succinctly states that the time to pull the guarantee is when its present value to the banks is minimal and the authorities have put in place provisions to control the public sector's exposure to the losses that banks incur.

To avoid premature removal, the supervisory agency and the central bank should both be prepared/ required to certify that the financial system is strong enough to withstand the strain of removing the guarantee. This certification must be based on reliable regulatory and market information about the current condition of the banking system and credible forecasts of its future condition. Second, legislation specifying the modalities of the system of deposit protection and efficient bank exit should be in place, and implementation plans should be virtually complete, before the date for removal is announced. Planning the reforms and passing the requisite legislation can easily take more than a year.

Moreover, it would be advisable to have contingency plans in place prior to removal in order to cover an unexpected loss of public confidence in individual banks or an unforeseen deterioration in banking industry conditions. For example, the lender of last resort may have to enlarge its support to help banks cope with transitional difficulties. The authorities should not revert to a full guarantee when faced with isolated banking problems or slow runs that can be dealt with under normal procedures. Instead, they should act decisively to cure ailing banks by prompt, corrective actions and merge, place in conservatorship, recapitalize, or liquidate insolvent banks.

Third, the authorities should be cautious in prematurely announcing a date for removal, especially at the time when the full guarantee is first put in place.[89] In fact, it may be necessary to announce a minimum time period during which the guarantee will remain in effect together with a minimum time period that will be given for the removal (as done in Indonesia). Some countries may wish to precommit to a date for removal to gain maximum credibility and to hasten the legislation and the structural reforms that need to accompany the removal of the guarantee.[90] The decision on when to remove a full guarantee must be examined on a country-by-country basis. If a general guarantee seems to stay in place too long, the development of a strategy for removal is imperative.

Recognizing that the guarantee should be removed as soon as possible, but facing a choice between removing the guarantee possibly prematurely and waiting for a very long time for ideal conditions to be met, some countries have chosen to phase out the guarantee over a period of time. Korea did so by reducing full coverage to principal, but not interest, for large deposits in August 1998. Mexico has already embarked on a complex schedule for removing its blanket guarantee by 2005. Sweden and Finland both removed their full guarantees once their financial systems had been restructured and they experienced no adverse effects. Japan initially announced that its blanket guarantee would be removed in 2001, but has subsequently extended the period for one year. Clearly, the authorities should move with determination to reform the financial system where necessary so that the preconditions can be met at the earliest opportunity.

Preparing for Removal

Even where it is not expected that the economy will be ready for the introduction of a system of limited protection for some time (perhaps several years), preparations for the transition need to be made in order to be consistent with the reforms that need to be made to banking and other laws. The date for the removal should be announced ahead of time to give the public time to adjust.

After Removal

After the guarantee is removed, the authorities need to demonstrate their commitment to the new arrangement and their determination not to backslide. A few precedent-setting actions by the authorities after the introduction of the system, such as disciplining troubled banks and resolving failed banks strictly according to the newly instituted rules, could confirm that the authorities will do what they have said they intend to do.

Phasing Out Full Guarantees on State-Owned Banks

A number of countries are currently considering how the authorities should deal with state-owned banks, including commercial, development, and savings banks whose deposits the government guarantees in full.[91] Similarly, they are considering whether and how to remove the guarantees on banks that are owned by municipalities or states.

The solution to this distortion is not to extend full depositor protection to other banks, but instead to subject the guaranteed bank to the same limited deposit guarantees (as well as prudential rules and supervision) that other banks receive. Any cutback in explicit deposit guarantees would have to be announced ahead of time and phased in (possibly over a long period) in order not to trigger runs and, possibly, a systemic crisis.

---

[89]Malaysia and Thailand have set no such deadlines. Mexico, Korea, and Japan have set target dates that have been, or may have to be, adjusted as the deadline approaches.

[90]Some analysts believe that setting a (realistic) date for removal is essential to drive needed reforms, and that waiting for the right time will delay action too long.

---

[91]Savings banks are guaranteed, for example, in the countries of the Commonwealth of Independent States and Sri Lanka.

In principle, there should be little hesitation in removing an implicit guarantee for state-owned and privately owned savings banks, especially where that guarantee lacks credibility. But even this situation presents a difficult choice for the authorities, who fear that removing even a shaky guarantee may precipitate runs. As for the removal of an explicit comprehensive guarantee, discussed above, the removal and its replacement with a limited system of deposit insurance needs to be timed correctly. That is, removal should occur after the banking system has been recapitalized and the system of supervision and regulation has been modified. This process can be expected to take time.

Some countries may choose to phase in removal by reducing coverage in successive steps down to the desired limit (Mexico has adopted this strategy). Other countries with a legal system that protects individuals' existing rights may have difficulty removing an existing guarantee for household deposits. The guarantee could then continue in place until a deposit is withdrawn, whereas new deposits would be insured under the new partial deposit insurance system.[92]

In some instances, guarantees have been given by other than the national authorities—for example, the state offers a full implicit guarantee for state-owned commercial banks and a local government provides an explicit guarantee for other segments of the industry. Either or both may lack credibility. In this situation, a noncredible guarantee should be replaced by a partial deposit guarantee that is temporarily confined to the relevant segments of the industry. A transfer of a guarantee from local to national authorities is not desirable. In the interim, any full implicit guarantee should remain in place for nationally owned banks until the state banks have been restructured. Then it can, and should, be replaced by a partial system that applies to all banks equally. The recommendations are similar when there is an explicit full guarantee for state-owned banks, but no coverage for privately owned institutions. That is, a limited system should be introduced first for banks with noncredible guarantees while retaining the full guarantee for state-owned banks until conditions are right for its replacement by the limited system.

Savings Banks

Removal of the guarantee is warranted but less urgent where a savings bank is already operating as a narrow bank that invests in safe government securities. It is less urgent because banks' yield structures would tend to reflect the different degrees of risk on their deposits. Savings banks with safe assets would pay lower deposit rates and not attract an inordinately large volume of deposits. Nevertheless, it is desirable to phase out such special treatment over time. Moreover, to the extent that a savings bank operates like any other commercial bank, or even transacts in the riskiest segments of the interbank market (as many of the savings banks in the CIS countries do), their guarantee constitutes a major distortion to the incentive and reward structure in place in the financial markets and should be removed as soon as can safely be accomplished.

Conclusions Regarding Removing Guarantees

As said above, a well-designed system of limited deposit insurance can foster stability in normal times. Although a full, explicit, temporary guarantee can be necessary in a systemic crisis, the guarantee should be removed as soon as is safely possible. A full guarantee should not be removed prematurely. When it is replaced by partial system of deposit insurance, small depositors should be covered and market discipline should be exercised by owners, where feasible, by holders of subordinated debt, and by a small number of uninsured large creditors and depositors (such as corporations and other financial institutions), supported by strong supervision and appropriate disclosure rules and internal controls. The option of distributing losses to large depositors and creditors is desirable in view of fiscal resource constraints and the desirability of sending strong signals to the market. Needless to say, this is inherently difficult.

---

[92]The full guarantee of household savings deposits made before 1993 is still in place in Hungary, although it now applies only to a minor amount of deposits. Deposits placed after 1993 have limited coverage.

V   Summary and Conclusions

Banks are vulnerable to illiquidity and insolvency. Because of banks' importance to the economy, most governments have chosen to implement a financial safety net to deal with such contingencies. A system of depositor protection that guards the holders of small deposits when their bank fails has in recent years become part of this safety net in a growing number of countries. A well-designed system of deposit insurance can strengthen incentives for good governance for banks (via strong internal governance from owners and managers, firm discipline from the markets, and effective bank supervision bank regulation).

Section II of the paper demonstrated how a well-designed deposit guarantee system can strengthen incentives for owners, managers, depositors and other creditors, borrowers, regulators and supervisors, and politicians. For instance, a well-designed system can promote good internal governance from owners and managers by disciplining weak banks, forcing the early closure of critically undercapitalized institutions, making membership compulsory, and charging risk-adjusted premiums. It can encourage market discipline by offering low coverage and disclosing good information that allows sophisticated depositors and other creditors to carefully monitor the condition of their bank. Borrowers should be aware that they will have to repay their loans if their bank fails and will be encouraged to keep their loans current where offsetting is limited to past-due loans. The performance of insurers, regulators and supervisors as agents will improve where they know that they can take justifiable actions without political interference and will be held accountable for their actions to their principals (depositors, taxpayers and/or bankers). Politicians will better serve the public good when they know that their actions will become public knowledge through disclosure laws that allow an inquisitive press to monitor compliance with the nation's conflict-of-interest laws.

The survey of current deposit insurance practices around the world shows that there is an increasing appreciation of the importance of system design. A larger proportion of systems of deposit protection are now explicit and compulsory, offer risk-adjusted premiums, are funded, have government backing, offer low coverage per depositor, and are government-run where taxpayer funds are at risk.

Nevertheless, there are still some areas of design and execution that need improvement. Coverage tends to be too high in low-income countries. Payment practices are slow, partly as a result of a trend toward excluding categories of deposits and depositors from coverage. Issues relating to what level of funding is adequate, how to equitably risk-adjust premiums, how to strike a balance between the roles of the government and the banking industry in running a system of deposit insurance require further study. The Financial Stability Forum's Working Group on Deposit Insurance will study these and other issues to improve the operation of deposit insurance systems around the world.

Despite these improvements, and possibly partly because there are issues in deposit insurance design that remain to be resolved, financial crises have been prevalent during the 1990s. This situation has forced a number of countries to offer a blanket guarantee to restore confidence and to allow the continued functioning of the financial system while the authorities take time to design a plan for the resolution of the crisis.

Should a systemic crisis occur, the government must assess the costs and benefits of imposing a full guarantee and decide whether the benefits exceed the costs. If it makes such an assessment, this paper outlines steps that the authorities can take to make the blanket guarantee effective, tailor it to fiscal reality, and ameliorate the damage it does to the incentive structure. Comprehensive coverage should be temporary, credibly funded, be replaced as soon as possible by an explicit limited system of deposit protection that follows good practice, and be accompanied by reform to the financial system to prevent a recurrence.

Bibliography

Akerlof, George A., and Paul M. Romer, 1993, "Looting: The Economic Underworld of Bankruptcy for Profit," *Brookings Papers on Economic Activity: 2*, Brookings Institution.

Alexander, William E., Jeffrey M. Davis, Liam P. Ebrill, and Carl-Johan Lindgren, 1997, *Systemic Bank Restructuring and Macroeconomic Policy* (Washington: International Monetary Fund).

Allen, Linda, and Anthony Saunders, 1993, "Forbearance and Valuation of Deposit insurance as a Callable Put," *Journal of Banking and Finance*, No.17, pp. 629–43.

Arzbach, Matthias, and Álvaro Durán, "Protección de Depósitos Bancarios en América Latina: Reformas Recientes y su Relevancia para Intermediarios Financieros," *Boletín* published by CEMLA (Centro de Estudios Monetarios Latinoamericanos), Mexico-City, Vol. XLIV, No. 6 (November–December 1998).

Baer, Herbert, and Daniela Klingebiel, 1995, "Systemic Risk when Depositor Bear Losses: Five Case Studies," in *Banking, Financial Market, and Systemic Risk*, Vol. 7 of *Research in Financial Services: Private and Public Policy*, ed. by George G. Kaufman (Greenwich, CT: JAI Press), pp. 195–302.

The Basle Committee on Banking Supervision, 1997, "Deposit Protection Schemes in Member Countries of the Basle Committee," *Compendium of Documents Produced by the Basle Committee on Banking Supervision* (Basle).

Beck, Thorsten, 2000, "Deposit Insurance as a Private Club: The Case of Germany." Paper presented at the World Bank Conference on Deposit Insurance (unpublished; Washington: World Bank).

Benston, George J., and George G. Kaufman, 1988, "Regulating Bank Safety and Performances," in *Restructuring Banking and Financial Services in America*," ed. by William S. Haraf and Rosemarie Kushmeider (Washington: American Enterprise Institute).

Board of Governors of the Federal Reserve System, 1999, *Using Subordinated Debt as an Instrument of Market Discipline,* Staff Study No. 172 (Washington: Board of Governors of the Federal Reserve System).

Demirguc-Kunt, Asli, and Enrica Detragiache, 1998, "The Determinants of Banking Crises in Developing and Developed Countries," *IMF Staff Papers*, Vol. 45, No. 1, pp. 81–109.

———, 1999, "Does Deposit Insurance Increase Banking System Stability?" World Bank Policy Research Working Paper, No. 247, (Washington: World Bank).

———, 2000, "Does Deposit Insurance Increase Banking System Stability?" IMF Working Paper 00/3 (Washington: International Monetary Fund).

Demirguc-Kunt, Asli, and H. Huizinga, 1999, "Market Discipline and Financial Safety Net Design," World Bank Policy Research Working Paper No. 283 (Washington: World Bank).

English, William B., 1993, "The Decline of Private Deposit Insurance in the United States," *Carnegie-Rochester Conference Series on Public Policy,* Vol. 93, pp. 57–128.

Enoch, Charles, Gillian Garcia, and V. Sundararajan, 1999, "Recapitalizing Banks with Public Funds: Selected Issues," IMF Working Paper 99/139 (Washington: International Monetary Fund).

European Union, May 30, 1994, "Directive 94/19/EC of the European Parliament and of the Council on Deposit Guarantee Schemes," *Official Journal of the European Communities*, No. L, pp. 135/5-12.

Flannery, Mark J., 1995, "Prudential Regulation for Banks," in *Financial Stability in a Changing Environment,* pp. 281–323 (New York: St. Martins Press).

Folkerts-Landau, David, and Carl-Johan Lindgren, 1998, *Toward a Framework for Financial Stability*, World Economic and Financial Surveys (Washington: International Monetary Fund).

Fries, Steven M., 1990, "Issues in the Reform of Deposit Insurance and the Regulation of Depository Institutions," IMF Working Paper 90/74 (Washington: International Monetary Fund).

———, and W.R.M. Perraudin, December 1991, "Banking Policy and the Pricing of Deposit Guarantees: A New Approach," IMF Working Paper 91/131, (Washington: International Monetary Fund).

Galbis, Vicente, December 1988, "Deposit Insurance: Policy Issues and Technical Aspects," IMF Central Banking Seminar (Washington: International Monetary Fund).

Garcia, Gillian, 1996, "Deposit Insurance: Obtaining the Benefits and Avoiding the Pitfalls," IMF Working Paper No. 96/83 (Washington: International Monetary Fund).

———, 1997a, *Protecting Bank Deposits*, Economic Issues Paper No. 9 (Washington: International Monetary Fund).

———, 1997b, "Depositor Protection and Banking Soundness," in *Banking Soundness and Monetary Policy: Issues and Experiences in the Global Economy,* ed.

by Charles Enoch and John H. Green (Washington: International Monetary Fund).

———, 1999, "Deposit Insurance: Actual and Best Practices," IMF Working Paper 99/54 (Washington: International Monetary Fund).

———, 2000, "Deposit Insurance and Crisis Management," IMF Working Paper 00/57 (Washington: International Monetary Fund).

———, and Elizabeth Plautz, 1988, *The Federal Reserve: Lender of Last Resort* (Cambridge: Harper Row).

Honohan Patrick, and Daniela Klingebiel, 2000, "Controlling Fiscal Costs of Banking Crises," Paper presented at the World Bank's Conference on Deposit Insurance (unpublished; Washington: World Bank).

Jackson, Patricia, 1996, "Depositor Protection and Bank Failures in the United Kingdom," *Financial Stability Review*, Vol. 1, pp. 38–43.

Kane, Edward J., 1989, *The S&L Insurance Mess: How Did It Happen?* (Washington: The Urban Institute Press).

———, 1992, "How Incentive-Incompatible Deposit-Insurance Funds Fail," *Journal of Financial Services Research,* Vol. 4. pp. 51–91.

———, 1995, "Three Paradigms for the Role of Capitalization Requirements in Insured Financial Institutions," *Journal of Banking and Finance*, Vol. 19, pp. 431–59.

Kaul, Inge, Isabelle Grunberg, and Marc A. Stern, 1999, "Concepts" in *Global Public Goods*, edited by Kaul, Inge, Isabelle Grunberg, and Marc A. Stern (New York: Oxford University Press).

Kydland, Finn, and Edward Prescott, 1977, "Rules Rather than Discretion: The Inconsistency of Optimal Plans," *Journal of Political Economy*, Vol. 85 (June), pp. 473–491.

Kyei, Alexander, 1995, "Deposit Protection Arrangements: A Comparative Study," IMF Working Paper 95/134 (Washington: International Monetary Fund).

Lang, William W., and Douglas Robertson, 2000, "Analysis of Proposals for a Minimum Subordinated Debt Requirement," U.S. Office of the Comptroller of the Currency, Economic and Policy Working Paper 00/04 (Washington).

Lindgren, Carl-Johan, and Gillian Garcia, 1996, "Deposit Insurance and Crisis Management," MAE Operational Paper No. 96/3, (Washington: International Monetary Fund).

———, and Matthew Saal, 1996, *Bank Soundness and Macroeconomic Policy* (Washington: International Monetary Fund).

Lindgren, Carl-Johan, Tomás J. T. Baliño, Charles Enoch, Anne-Marie Gulde, Marc Quintyn, and Leslie Teo, 2000, *Financial Sector Crisis and Restructuring: Lessons from Asia*, IMF Occasional Paper No. 188 (Washington: International Monetary Fund).

McCarthy, Ian S., 1980, "Deposit Insurance: Theory and Practice," *Staff Papers*, International Monetary Fund, Vol. 27 (September), pp. 578–600.

Merton, Robert C., and Zvi Bodie, 1993, "Deposit Insurance Reform: A Functional Approach," *Carnegie-Rochester Conference Series on Public Policy. 38.*

Netherlands, 1996, *The Law of the Kingdom of the Netherlands on Bankruptcy.*

Peltzman, Sam, 1976, "Toward a More General Theory of Regulation," *Journal of Law and Economics*, Vol. 19 (June), pp. 152–66.

Pennachi, George G., 1987, "Alternative Forms of Deposit Insurance: Pricing and Incentive Issues," *Journal of Banking and Finance,* Vol. 11, pp. 291–312.

———, 1987, "A Reexamination of the Over-(Or Under-) Pricing of Deposit Insurance," *Journal of Money, Credit and Banking,* Vol. 19, pp. 340–360.

Posner, Richard A., 1974, "Theories of Economic Regulation," *Bell Journal of Economics and Management Science*, Vol. 5, No. 2, pp. 335–58.

Saunders, Anthony, 1994, *Financial Institutions Management: A Modern Perspective, (Richard D. Irwin Inc. Burn Ridge, Illinois).*

Sundararajan, V., and Tomás J.T. Baliño, 1991, *Banking Crises: Cases and Issues*, ed. (Washington: International Monetary Fund).

Talley, Samuel H., and Ignacio Mas, 1990, "Deposit Insurance in Developing Countries," World Bank Policy Research and External Affairs Working Paper No. 548 (Washington: World Bank).

United States, Federal Deposit Insurance Corporation, 1996, *Manual of Policies and* Procedures for Bank Liquidation and Receivership (Washington: FDIC).

United States, House of Representatives, 1991, *Federal Deposit Insurance Corporation Improvement Act of 1991:* Report to Accompany H.R. 3768 (Washington: U.S. House of Representatives).

Wood, Philip R., 1995, *Principles of International Insolvency,* (London: Sweet and Maxwell).

Wyplosz, Charles, 1999, "International Financial Instability," in *Global Public Goods,* ed. by Inge Kaul, Isabelle Grunberg, and Marc A. Stern (New York: Oxford University Press).

Statistical Appendix

Table A1. Depositor Protection Schemes Explicitly Defined: Membership and Nature of the Deposit Insurance System

Region, Country or Province	Membership			Responsibilities of the System (broad or narrow)
	Date enacted/revised	Compulsory	Voluntary	
AFRICA				
Cameroon[1]	1999		X	Narrow.
Central African Republic[1]			X	Narrow.
Chad[1]	2000		X	Narrow.
Congo, Republic[1]			X	Narrow.
Equatorial Guinea[1]			X	Narrow.
Gabon[1]			X	Narrow.
Kenya	1985	X		Broad.
Nigeria	1988/89	X		Broad.
Tanzania	1994	X		Broad.
Uganda	1994	X		Narrow.
Zambia	Proposed, but not implemented.			
ASIA				
Bangladesh	1984/2000 pending.	X		Narrow.
Hong Kong SAR	Hong Kong considered and rejected installing a deposit insurance system in 1992; but is currently reconsidering.			
India	1961	X		Narrow, considering broadening.
Japan[2]	1971 (in full since 1995/96)	X		Broad.
Indonesia	1998 (A full, explicit guarantee was introduced in 1998).			
Kazakhstan	1999	X		Narrow.
Korea[3]	1996 (currently in full)	X		Broad.
Malaysia	A full guarantee was introduced in December 1997.			
Marshall Islands[4]	1975		X	Broad.
Micronesia[5]	1963		X	Broad.
Philippines	1963	X		Broad.
Sri Lanka	1987		X	Narrow.
Thailand	In full since 1997, but a draft law is under consideration to replace the full guarantee.			
Taiwan Province of China	1985/95/99	X (since 2/99)		Broad.
EUROPE				
Albania	Under consideration.			
Austria	1979/96	X		Narrow.
Belgium	1974/95	X		Broad.
Bulgaria	1998	X		Narrow (is considering broadening).
Croatia	1997/99	X		Broad.
Czech Republic	1994	X		Narrow.
Denmark	1988/98	X		Narrow.
Estonia	1998	X		Narrow.
Finland[6]	1969/92/98	X		Narrow.
France[7]	1980/95/99	X		Narrow.
Germany[8]	1966/76/98	X (official)	X (private)	Narrow.
Gibraltar	1998	X		Narrow.
Greece	1993/95	X		Narrow.
Hungary	1993	X		Broad.
Iceland[9]	1985/96/2000	X		Narrow.

Table A1 *(continued)*

Region, Country or Province	Membership			Responsibilities of the System
	Date enacted/revised	Compulsory	Voluntary	(broad or narrow)
Ireland	1989/95	X		Broad.
Italy[10]	1987/96/99	X		Broad.
Latvia	1998	X		Narrow.
Lithuania	1996	X		Narrow.
Luxembourg	1989/99	X		Narrow.
Macedonia	1996/97/98/00	X		Narrow.
Netherlands	1979/95	X		Narrow.
Norway[11]	1961/97	X		Broad.
Poland[12]	1995	X		Broad.
Portugal	1992/95	X		Narrow.
Romania	1996	X		Narrow.
Russia	A draft law was passed by the Parliament but vetoed by the President in 2000. There is an implicit guarantee of household deposits in the savings bank.			
Slovak Republic	1996	X		Narrow.
Spain[13]	1977/96	X		Broad.
Sweden[14]	1996	X		Narrow.
Switzerland	1984/93		X	Narrow.
Turkey[15]	1983 (in full since December 1999).	X		Narrow.
Ukraine	1998	X		Narrow.
United Kingdom	1982/95	X		Narrow.
MIDDLE EAST				
Bahrain	1993	X		Narrow.
Israel	Implicit-the central bank has compensated all depositors in full for the last 30 years.			
Kuwait	Implicit: Kuwait is beginning to consider a formal scheme.			
Lebanon	1967/91	X		Narrow.
Morocco	1993/96[16]	X		Broad.
Oman	1995	X		Broad.
WESTERN HEMISPHERE				
Argentina	1971/95	X		Broad in principle.
Bahamas	1999	X		Broad.
Bolivia	Deposit insurance system proposed in 1999 but not yet enacted.			
Brazil	1974/81/95	X (de facto)		Narrow.
Canada	1967/95	X		Broad.
Chile[17]	1986	X		Broad.
Colombia	1985	X		Broad since 1998.
Costa Rica[18]	There is an explicit full guarantee, but only for state-owned banks. An explicit, limited scheme is under discussion for both state-owned and private banks.			
Dominican Republic[19]	1962/99		X	Narrow.
Ecuador	July 1998. In full December 1998.[20]	X		Broad.
El Salvador[21]	1991/2000	X		Broad.
Guatemala	1999	X		Narrow.
Honduras	1999/2000 (in full until 2002).	X		Broad.
Jamaica[22]	1998 (full from 1997 to 1998).	X		Broad.
Mexico[23]	1986/90/99 (full: beginning to be phased out).	X		Broad.

Table A1 *(concluded)*

Region, Country or Province	Membership			Responsibilities of the System (broad or narrow)
	Date enacted/revised	Compulsory	Voluntary	
Panama	Has explicit coverage only for credit cooperatives.			
Peru	1992/99	X		Broad.[24]
Trinidad & Tobago	1986	X		Broad.
United States[25]	1934/91	X[26]		Broad.
Venezuela	1985	X		Broad.
Number of Countries Examined: 85	72 countries offer an explicit deposit insurance system; the guarantee is in full in 11 countries.	62 Schemes[27]	7 Schemes[27]	Narrow role in 34 countries; Broad responsibilities in 33 systems.

Sources: Information provided by country authorities; and IMF staff.

Notes: ... Means data are not available.

[1]The format for the establishment of a system of deposit insurance has been adopted by six central African countries that share a central bank (Cameroon, Central African Republic, Chad, Republic of Congo, Equatorial Guinea, and Gabon). The treaty that embodies the system has been ratified by Cameroon and Chad. Ratification is pending elsewhere. The scheme will not go into operation until all regional members have ratified the treaty.

[2]Japan has two systems. The first covers, commercial and shinkin banks, which are credit cooperatives, and labor and credit associations but the authorities have extended a temporary full guarantee. The second scheme covers agricultural and fishery cooperatives.

[3]Korea has placed a temporary full guarantee on deposits.

[4]Two U.S. banks in the Marshall Islands are insured by the United Sates' FDIC under special U.S. legislation, but the domestic bank is not covered.

[5]Banks in Micronesia are insured by the United States' FDIC under special U.S. legislation.

[6]Finland has a relatively new system that replaces its comprehensive guarantee.

[7]France has separate schemes for commercial banks and for mutual, savings and cooperative banks.

[8]Germany has both public and private schemes. There are separate private schemes for commercial banks, savings banks, giro institutions, and credit cooperatives. Since August 1998 there has been in place an official compulsory scheme for commercial banks. The private scheme supplements the public deposit insurance system by covering the 10 percent deductible and topping up coverage. The private deposit insurance system can assist troubled banks.

[9]Until January 2000, Iceland had two schemes for deposit protection-one for commercial banks and the other for savings banks. Both are monitored by the supervisory agency. The two schemes have now been merged.

[10]Italy has two separate schemes, one for commercial banks (that have 90 percent of the system's deposits) and the other for smaller, mutual institutions.

[11]Norway has two separate deposit insurance funds-one for commercial banks and the other for savings banks..

[12]Poland has three separate schemes.

[13]There are three separate systems in Spain: one for commercial banks, a second for savings banks, and the third for credit cooperatives. They are similar in composition.

[14]Before its banking crisis, Sweden did not have a system of depositor protection. It introduced a temporary guarantee of all bank liabilities in 1992, and replaced it with a formal system of deposit insurance to conform to EU standards in January 1996 for all banks and investment firms that receive deposits.

[15]Turkey explicitly insures savings deposits and CDs, but in 1994, it extended an implicit guarantee to all deposits.

[16]The legislation setting up the deposit insurance system in Morocco was enacted in 1993; however, the Ministry of Finance was required to approve the by-laws and did not do so until 1996.

[17]In Chile, the central bank guarantees demand deposits. The government guarantees 90 percent of household savings and time deposits to a limit of UF 120 per person per year, that is, 120 inflation-adjusted units of Chilean currency.

[18]Article 4 of the Banking Law in Costa Rica states that state-owned banks can count on a guarantee from the government. The public has interpreted this article as providing unlimited deposit protection at state-owned banks.

[19]The Dominican Republic currently has explicit deposit insurance only for savings and loan associations and the National Housing Bank. A law giving wider deposit protection in the form of legal priority passed the legislature in 1999, but was vetoed by the President.

[20]A deposit insurance system was enacted in Ecuador in July 1998, but was temporarily over-ridden by a full guarantee that was placed in December 1998. However, deposits were frozen in March 1999 and will be repaid mostly in government bonds as dollarization precludes creating new money.

[21]El Salvador is implementing a new deposit insurance system that covers most deposits.

[22]Jamaica instituted an explicit full guarantee in 1995. A limited deposit insurance system was enacted in March 1998 and began operations in September 1998.

[23]Mexico did not impose an obligation on its insurance agency (FOBAPROA) to guarantee deposits, but each December, the agency announced what instruments it would cover. For example, in 1997, it stated that it would cover all liabilities of commercial banks except subordinated debt. A new law was passed in 1998 under which a new agency, IPAB, insures deposits. The full guarantee is being phased out-a process to be completed by year 2005.

[24]The system in Peru was granted a broad role in the revised legislation of 1999.

[25]The United States has three separate schemes: one for commercial banks, a second for savings associations, and a third for credit unions. Deposits booked offshore are not covered.

[26]Deposit insurance in the United States is compulsory for nationally chartered banks, for state-chartered banks that are members of the Federal Reserve System and for other banks where their state charters require it. In short, federal insurance is compulsory for virtually all bank and thrifts.

[27]The numbers of compulsory and voluntary schemes exceed the total of 68 because Germany has both public and private schemes that are characterized differently.

Table A2. Membership in Explicit Limited Deposit Insurance Systems

Region, Country or Province	Institutional Membership	Participation by the Branches of Foreign Banks	Cover for Domestic Banks' Branches Abroad
AFRICA			
Kenya	...	Voluntary.	Voluntary.
Nigeria	Licensed banks.		
Tanzania	All licensed banks, including the Tanzania Postal Bank, and financial institutions that take deposits.	Yes.	
Uganda	Commercial banks.		
ASIA			
Bangladesh	All scheduled private, foreign, and Islamic financial institutions.	Yes.	
India	Commercial, cooperative and rural banks that are either publicly or privately owned.	Yes.	No.
Japan	Commercial, trust, long-term credit and shinkin banks, credit cooperatives, labor and credit associations. A separate scheme covers agricultural and credit cooperatives. Government-related institutions and branches of foreign banks are not covered.	No.	Not normally.
Kazakhstan	Banks licensed to accept deposits and that have met international prudential standards.	Yes.	
Korea	Under full coverage: national and regional commercial banks, specialized banks, the Korea Development and Long-term Credit Banks, and branches of foreign banks.	Yes.	Yes.
Marshall Is.	Branches of U.S. commercial banks.	Yes.	
Micronesia	Commercial banks.	Yes.	
Philippines	All institutions granted a banking license.	Yes.	
Sri Lanka	Registered banking institutions and cooperative societies carrying on banking business. A new, separate, cross-guarantee, scheme for cooperative societies was initiated in 1999.	Voluntary.	
Taiwan Province of China	All financial institutions licensed to accept deposits or trust funds.	Compulsory, unless covered equivalently by a home-country deposit insurance system.	
EUROPE			
Austria	Credit institutions that take deposits.	Compulsory for non-EU banks. EU banks may opt to "top up."	Yes, for EU members.
Belgium	Licensed credit institutions.	Compulsory (unless the home country has an equivalent scheme).	Yes (unless the host country has an equivalent scheme).
Bulgaria	All banks legally licensed to take deposits.	Compulsory (unless the home country has an equivalent scheme).	No.
Croatia	Commercial and savings banks, but not savings and loan associations.	Compulsory (unless the home country has an equivalent scheme).	No.
Czech Republic	All licensed banks and the branches and agencies of foreign banks.	Yes.	No.
Denmark	Commercial, savings and cooperative banks and the branches of foreign banks.	Compulsory for banks from non-EU countries unless they have comparable coverage, then voluntary.	Yes.

Table A2 *(continued)*

Region, Country or Province	Institutional Membership	Participation by the Branches of Foreign Banks	Cover for Domestic Banks' Branches Abroad
Estonia	Credit institutions.	Yes, unless covered by a comparable scheme from home.	No
Finland		Voluntary.	No.
France	All licensed credit institutions since July 1999. (There had previously been a separate scheme for mutual, savings and cooperative banks.)	Compulsory.	Yes (but only for EEA countries).
Germany	The official deposit insurance system covers all licensed banking institutions. There are also separate private schemes for commercial banks, savings banks and credit cooperatives.	Voluntary (although all branches in fact participate in the scheme).	Yes: for German banks operating in EU countries. The private sector covers all branches.
Gibraltar	Banks incorporated in Gibraltar, offices from banks from non-EEA countries that are authorized to operate in Gibraltar.[1]	Voluntary for EU banks to "top up" coverage. Compulsory for non-EU banks lacking comparable coverage.	No.
Greece	All credit institutions authorized to conduct banking business in Greece except for the Postal Savings Bank, the Deposit and Loan Fund, and credit cooperatives.	Compulsory (unless the home country has an equivalent scheme).	Yes (unless the host country has an equivalent scheme).
Hungary	All types of licensed financial institutions, except state-guaranteed institutions and credit cooperatives.	Yes.	
Iceland	Until January 2000, Iceland had two separate deposit insurance systems-one for commercial banks and the other for savings banks. They have now been combined.		
Ireland	All authorized credit institutions, including building societies.	Compulsory, except for credit institutions authorized in another EEA country.	No, except within the EEA.
Italy	There are two separate deposit insurance systems, one for commercial banks and the other for smaller mutual and cooperative institutions.	Voluntary.	Yes, for EU (unless the host country has an equivalent scheme).
Latvia	All banks authorized to accept deposits from natural persons.	...	No.
Lithuania	Lithuanian commercial banks and state banks where the state holds less than 50% of the shares,	...	No.
Luxembourg	All institutions licensed to accept deposits.	Compulsory.	No.
Macedonia	Banks and savings houses in Macedonia and branches of foreign banks registered in Macedonia.	Yes, voluntary,	No.
Netherlands	All financial institutions licensed to take deposits.	Compulsory.	No.
Norway	There are separate schemes for commercial banks and savings banks.		
Poland	All banks operating in Poland, except for cooperative banks, which have a separate scheme.	Yes.	No.
Portugal	Credit institutions that have their head office in Portugal and are authorized to take deposits and branches of non-EU banks.	Compulsory (unless the home country has an equivalent scheme). EU banks may "top up" their home coverage.	No.
Romania			
Slovak Republic	Commercial banks and building societies.		
Spain	All Spanish credit institutions included in the Register of Banks. There are three separate schemes: one for commercial banks, one for savings banks, and one for credit cooperatives.	Voluntary.	Yes (only for EEA countries).

Table A2 *(continued)*

Region, Country or Province	Institutional Membership	Participation by the Branches of Foreign Banks	Cover for Domestic Banks' Branches Abroad
Sweden	All Swedish and foreign commercial banks and all investment firms that are licensed to accept deposits.	Voluntary for EEA and non-EEA banks (if the home country has an equivalent scheme).	Yes (voluntary for branches in EEA countries and possible with the permission of the deposit insurance system for branches elsewhere.
Switzerland	All banks operating in Switzerland, i.e. members of the Swiss Bankers' Association.	Yes.	No.
Turkey	Normally banks licensed to take household savings deposits.		
Ukraine	Licensed commercial banks that are included in the National Bank of Ukraine's Register of Banks. The Savings Bank of Ukraine is not a member.	Yes.	No.
United Kingdom	Banks licensed to take deposits and incorporated in the United Kingdom, non-EEA incorporated banks that are authorized to take deposits through UK offices, and branches of UK incorporated banks in the EEA. Building societies have a separate scheme.	Compulsory for branches on non-EEA banks operating in the UK, unless they can prove they have a comparable home scheme. Voluntary for branches of EEA banks "topping up" cover.	Yes for branches of UK incorporated banks operating in the EEA.
MIDDLE EAST			
Bahrain	Bahraini offices of full commercial banks.	Yes, unless covered by a similar scheme elsewhere.	Yes.
Lebanon	All banks existing and operating in Lebanon.	Yes.	Yes.
Morocco	"All credit institutions receiving public funds."	No.	No.
Oman	Banks licensed by the central bank to accept deposits and are operating in Oman.	...	No.
WESTERN HEMISPHERE			
Argentina	Commercial banks, savings banks, and credit unions, if they are supervised.[2]	Yes.	No.
Bahamas	Every licensed bank conducting business in Bahamian currency.	Yes.	
Brazil	Financial institutions, including savings and credit associations that accept deposits, but not credit cooperatives.	Yes.	No.
Canada	Domestic banks and subsidiaries, domestic trust and loan companies, foreign bank subsidiaries.	Yes.	No.
Chile	Commercial banks and savings banks of all types, but not credit cooperatives.	Yes.	No.
Colombia	All entities that take deposits, including banks, finance companies, savings associations, leasing companies and investment trusts. There is a separate scheme for credit cooperatives.	Yes.	No.
Dominican Republic	Savings and loan associations and the National Housing Bank. The draft law would extend protection to all banking institutions.	Yes.	No.
Ecuador	Commercial banks, savings banks and credit cooperatives that are supervised.	Yes.	Yes.
El Salvador	All banks, except two state-owned banks, but not credit cooperatives.	Yes, unless they are insured by the home country.	Yes.
Guatemala	Private domestic banks and branches of foreign banks.	Yes.	

Table A2 *(concluded)*

Region, Country or Province	Institutional Membership	Participation by the Branches of Foreign Banks	Cover for Domestic Banks' Branches Abroad
Honduras	Private banks, savings and loan associations, finance companies, foreign banks authorized to accept deposits.	Yes.	
Jamaica	All financial institutions licensed to accept deposits.	Yes.	No.
Mexico	Full service commercial banks, but not savings or credit cooperatives.		
Peru	All commercial banks and certain other financial institutions that are supervised and authorized to accept deposits.	Yes.	No.
Trinidad & Tobago	All licensed financial institutions, including commercial banks, finance houses, trust companies, and merchant banks.	Yes.	No.
United States	Commercial and savings banks are insured by the Bank Insurance Fund. (There are separate funds for savings associations and credit unions.)	No, they have to be subsidiaries.	No (except for U.S. banks in the Marshall Islands and Micronesia and unless the deposits are payable in the United States).
Venezuela	Commercial and other banks that are supervised.		
67 Countries normally have an explicit, limited DIS*	Typically included are financial institutions licensed to take deposits.	Yes: 40 Voluntary: 8	No: 30 Yes: within the EEA and 5 other countries.

Sources: Country authorities; and IMF staff.

Notes: . . . Means data are not available.

* Excluding the scheme for credit cooperatives in Panama.

[1]Countries in the EEA are Austria, Belgium, Denmark, Finland, France, Germany, Greece, Iceland, Ireland, Italy, Liechtenstein, Luxembourg, the Netherlands, Norway, Portugal, Spain, Sweden, and the United Kingdom.

[2]In Argentina in 2000, only commercial banks are covered because other banks are excluded because they pay excessively high rates on their deposits.

Table A3. Private and Official Funding for Explicit Limited Deposit Insurance Systems

Region, Country or Province	Has Private Funding[1]	Has Official Backing[2]	Fund or Ex Post Assessment	Investing Fund Resources	Legal Priority for Depositors or the Deposit Insurance System
AFRICA					
Kenya	X	Central bank can make loans.	Fund.		No.
Nigeria	X	Government (the ministry of finance and central bank) provided initial capital and can make loans.	Fund.	Mainly Nigerian T-bills.	Yes, de jure.
Tanzania	X	The government provided initial capital and the central bank can make loans.	Fund.	Tanzanian T-bills and loans to banks.	No, de jure, at par with other creditors.
Uganda	X	Government provided initial capital and will lend.	Fund.		Yes.
ASIA					
Bangladesh	X	Deposit insurance agency finances are co-mingled within the central bank. They would be separated under pending legislation and the deposit insurer could borrow from the central bank.	Fund.	Approved, risk-free securities and investments.	Yes.
India	X	The central bank provided initial capital. It and government give support with Parliamentary approval.	Fund.	Indian central government securities.	No, at par with unsecured creditors.
Japan	X	Government and central bank provided initial capital. The central bank makes loans. The government has provided substantial assistance.	Fund.	Central and local government securities and corporate bonds.	No.
Kazakhstan	X	The deposit insurance system can borrow from the government and the central bank.	Fund.	Government securities.	Yes.
Korea	X	The KDIC is legally authorized to borrow from the government or central bank with ministry of finance approval.	Fund.	...	No.
Marshall Is.	X		Fund.	US government securities.	Yes.
Micronesia	X		Fund.	US government securities.	Yes.
Philippines	X	The government provided initial capital, central bank made loans and has borne losses.	Fund.	...	Yes: the PDIC has priority for insured deposits.
Sri Lanka	X	The central bank provided initial capital and has advanced funds.	Fund.	...	No.
Taiwan Province of China	X	The government provided initial capital. The central bank makes loans against collateral or a guarantee from the ministry of finance.	Fund.	Cash, securities, government bonds, and bank debentures.	No.
EUROPE					
Austria	X	Government-guaranteed bonds may be issued.	Ex post.	Not relevant.	Yes: for small depositors.
Belgium	X	The state has provided a limited temporary guarantee.	Fund.	...	No.
Bulgaria	X	Fund has the right to borrow, including from the government in the last resort, and to receive donations and foreign assistance.	Fund.	...	Yes, for the deposit insurer.
Croatia	X	The fund may borrow from the central bank.	Fund.	Short-term government and central bank securities.	Yes, for insured deposits.
Czech Republic	X	The central bank and the government would equally make loans to cover any shortfall in funding.	Fund.	...	No.
Denmark	X	The deposit insurer can borrow from banks with a guarantee from the government.	Fund.	...	No.
Estonia	X	The government made an initial contribution. The fund can borrow without a government guarantee or ask the government to borrow a limited amount on its behalf.	Fund.	OECD-country bonds, deposits of non-member credit institutions.	No.
Finland	X	The government and the central bank have borne losses. The fund can borrow with a government guarantee.	Fund.		No.

Table A3 (continued)

Region, Country or Province	Has Private Funding[1]	Has Official Backing[2]	Fund or Ex Post Assessment	Investing Fund Resources	Legal Priority for Depositors or the Deposit Insurance System
France	X	The Government re-capitalized Credit Lyonnais outside the deposit insurance system. Both the old and the new deposit insurance systems are funded solely from private sources.	Fund beginning in 1999.	...	No.
Germany	X	Local governments have supported the scheme for savings institutions. Other schemes can borrow, but the law requires that compensation under the public scheme be paid from members' annual supplementary contributions.	Fund (ex post for one private system).	...	No.
Gibraltar	X	None.	Ex post (fund for admin. expenses).	Not relevant.	No.
Greece	X	Sixty percent of the start-up funding was provided by the central bank.	Fund.	80% in members' CDs, 20% government paper.	...
Hungary	X	The government will guarantee fund borrowing from the central bank or private markets if requested.	Fund.	Hungarian government bonds, credit institution deposits.	Yes, for private persons' deposits.
Iceland[5]	X	No support.	Fund.	...	No.
Ireland	X	...	Fund.	...	No.
Italy	X	Under the Legge Decree, the Bank of Italy can make low-interest rate loans to facilitate a large pay-out. The government has recently provided substantial financial assistance to the deposit insurance system.	Only for admin. expenses (thinking of changing).	Not relevant.	Yes: insurer has priority for insured deposits.
Latvia	X	The Bank of Latvia and the government made initial contributions. Compensation is paid from the government's budget if fund resources are inadequate.	Fund.	Latvian government securities.	Yes, de jure.
Lithuania	X	The government provided initial capital and will cover any shortfall with loans.[3]	Fund.	...	Yes, for insured deposits.
Luxembourg	X	...	Ex post.	Not relevant.	...
Macedonia	X	The central bank can extend credit if the fund lacks resources to pay insured depositors.	Fund.	Securities issued by the central bank.	Yes, for insured deposits.
Netherlands	X	The central bank provides interest-free bridge financing.	Ex post.	Not relevant.	No.
Norway	X	Government and central bank have borne losses. The government created a Government Bank Insurance Fund to make loans to the Commercial Bank and the Savings Bank Guarantee Funds, whose resources had been depleted by the banking crisis.	Fund.	...	Yes, if the bank is under public administration.
Poland	X	The Bank of Poland and the government contributed initial capital.	Fund.	Assistance loans to banks and government securities.[4]	Yes: the insurer has priority.
Portugal	X	The Bank of Portugal provided initial capital.	Fund.	Assets agreed with the central bank.	No.
Romania	X	The fund can borrow from the state, the central bank, and other sources. The government can guarantee the debt.	Fund.	Romanian T-bills.	No.
Slovak Republic	X	The central bank made an initial contribution and may make loans.	Fund.	...	No.
Spain	X	The central bank can make limited loans.	Fund.	Interest-bearing account at the National Debt Office.	No.
Sweden	X	The government has borne losses. The deposit insurer may borrow from the National Debt Office.	Fund.	...	No.

Table A3 (continued)

Region, Country or Province	Has Private Funding[1]	Has Official Backing[2]	Fund or Ex Post Assessment	Investing Fund Resources	Legal Priority for Depositors or the Deposit Insurance System
Switzerland	X	No. The Swiss Banker's Association borrows under normal market conditions.	Ex post.	Not relevant.	Yes, for insured depositors.
Turkey	X	Credit may be extended by the central bank in case of insufficiency in funding.	Fund.	In banks to obtain high yields.	Yes, de jure.
Ukraine	X	The government made an initial contribution through the National Bank of the Ukraine. The deposit insurer can borrow from the government.	Fund.	Ukrainian government securities.	Yes, for the deposit insurer.
United Kingdom	X	The central bank made loans in the past but there is now no public funding for the deposit insurance system, but it may borrow limited amounts in the markets with Treasury approval.	Small fund (£5m to £6m) mainly ex post.	Yes, the deposit insurance agency has priority in recoveries	Treasury bills for the small fund.
MIDDLE EAST					
Bahrain	X	The new law would allow the deposit insurance system to borrow from the markets or the central bank.	Ex post, currently.[5]	Not relevant.	No.
Lebanon	X	The central bank contributed half of the deposit insurance system's initial capital. The government matches banks' annual contributions. If the fund is depleted the central bank replenishes it by making interest-free loans.	Fund.	Lebanese T-bills, bonds and real estate in Lebanon.	...
Morocco	X	No public support was used to establish the deposit insurance system and nonpublic monies are provided for in the legislation.[6]	Fund.	Negotiable securities of the Moroccan government.	No.
Oman	X	The central bank matched half of the member banks' initial contributions; the fund can borrow from the Government, the central bank and member banks.	Fund.	Must consider: risk, liquidity, and revenue.	Yes, for the deposit insurer.
WESTERN HEMISPHERE					
Argentina	X	The central bank contributed a small share of the initial capital.	Fund.	Abroad.	Yes.
Bahamas	X	The central bank contributed half the deposit insurance system's initial capital.	Fund.	...	Yes: the deposit insurance system has priority for insured deposits.
Brazil	X	The deposit insurance system can either request funds from the central bank or authorization to borrow. Under the constitution no government support is available.	Fund.	A private decision.	No.
Canada	X	The fund can borrow from the markets and the government, but is charged private market rates.[7]	Fund.[7]	...	No, same rank as unsecured creditors.
Chile	No	The government is responsible for time and savings deposits and the central bank for demand deposits.	Government.	Government securities.	Yes, for insured depositors.
Colombia	X	It is understood that the state is the ultimate guarantor.	Fund.	Colombian government securities.	No.
Dominican Republic	X	The government can fund the deposit insurance system for savings and loan associations.	Fund.	...	Yes, by law in 1999.
Ecuador	X	Until December 1999, the fund could request the central bank to provide liquidity to a bank in rehabilitation. The deposit insurance system also received government bonds from the ministry of finance. However, under the dollarization scheme, no new money can be created. As the deposit insurance system has run out of cash, deposits have been frozen since March 1999, and must be repaid by government bonds.	Fund.	The deposit insurance system uses the same criteria as for investing international reserves.	Yes: same as for public deposits.

Table A3 (concluded)

Region, Country or Province	Has Private Funding[1]	Has Official Backing[2]	Fund or Ex Post Assessment	Investing Fund Resources	Legal Priority for Depositors or the Deposit Insurance System
El Salvador	X	The central bank provided initial funding and it may also make loans to the deposit insurance system.	Fund.	Securities at home and abroad, foreign bank deposits, considering risk and liquidity.	No.
Guatemala	X	The government may make a temporary, exceptional contribution, which is to be repaid by the banks later.	Fund.	Foreign or domestic, non-member institutions; to consider security, profitability, liquidity, and diversification.	Yes.
Honduras	X	The government made an initial contribution, which may be repaid over time. The central bank has a contingent credit line for the deposit insurance system; the ministry of finance may issue bonds.	Fund.	A special fund at the central bank.	No.
Jamaica	X	The fund can borrow in the markets or from the government and has an explicit government guarantee.	Fund.	Jamaican or foreign-government securities or banks.	No.
Mexico	X	Fund has borrowed from the central bank and ministry of finance.	Fund.	Liquid government securities.	Yes.
Peru	X	The central bank and the Treasury made initial contributions. Fund may borrow from the Treasury.	Fund.	Central bank and corporate securities, including foreign currency or government securities, bonds, mutual funds, but not Peruvian finance companies-to consider: security, liquidity, profitability and diversification.	No.
Trinidad & Tobago	X	Central bank made an initial contribution, matches banks' contributions, and may lend to the fund.	Fund.	Cash and the marketable securities of domestic or foreign governments.	Yes, the deposit insurance system has priority for insured deposits.
United States	X	Government provided initial capital, bore S&L losses, and can lend to BIF and SAIF.	Fund.	Special issue U.S. government securities.	Yes.
Venezuela	X	Central bank and government have borne losses and refinanced FOGADE, the deposit insurance system. The central bank may make advances.	Fund.	Securities that are liquid and profitable, equity interests.	Yes, for small deposits.
67 countries normally have an explicit, limited systems of deposit insurance*	66 systems have some or all private funds, one is funded by government.	Funds in 55 countries have received government assistance or can expect to obtain it. Five countries deny that support will be provided. The situation is unclear in the remaining countries.	58 systems build a fund and 9 rely mainly on ex post levies.	Typically domestic government securities.	Yes: 31, No: 30, No information: 8

Sources: Country authorities; and IMF staff.

Notes: ... Means data are not available.

*Excluding the scheme for credit cooperatives in Panama.

[1]Funding reflects the ongoing responsibility to contribute to an insurance fund or to pay ex post assessments in order to compensate depositors of a failed bank. Situations where the government has provided initial funding, has an obligation to supply loans, or has borne losses are also indicated in column 3.

[2]The government should be understood to include the central bank in determining official support for funding.

[3]Resources from the government were needed in Lithuania to fund the system, which was expected to be fully funded from bank premiums starting in 1999.

[4]In Poland, foreign banks retain their premiums until they are needed by the deposit insurance system.

[5]The draft law in Bahrain provides for a fund, with contributions to be shared between the government and the banks.

[6]If the fund proves to be insufficient in Morocco, depositor compensation is reduced pro rata.

[7]The law in Canada does not require the CDIC to accumulate a fund. Instead, it puts aside provisions to cover expected future losses and accumulates them in a reserve (typically called an allowance for loan losses (ALL)). Currently, the CDIC has resources that exceed the ALL.

Table A4. Building the Fund in an Explicit Limited Deposit Insurance System

Region, Country, or Province	Fund Target as a Percent of Deposits	Actual Fund as a Percent of Deposits	Premium or Assessment Base	Annual Premium as a Percentage of the Assessment Base	Basis for Risk-Adjusting Premiums[1]
AFRICA					
Kenya	20% of insured deposits.	5.3% insured deposits.	Deposits.	0.15	
Nigeria	Not specified.	...	Deposits.	0.9375	
Tanzania	3% of total deposits.[2]	2.7% of total deposits.	Deposits.	0.1	
Uganda	No.	Reported to be very low.	Deposits.	0.2	
ASIA					
Bangladesh	...	0.4% of insured deposits.	Deposits.	0.005	
India	No, but 2% has been proposed.	0.7% of insured deposits.	Deposits.	0.05	
Japan	No.	Currently has a deficit.	Insured deposits.	0.048 + 0.036	
Kazakhstan	Yes T 500 million.	New scheme.	Insurable deposits.	Risk-based: 0.125 to 0.375	Formula reflecting financial condition.
Korea	...	...	Deposits.	0.05	
Marshall Islands	U.S. system.	U.S. system.	Deposits.	Risk-based: 0.00 to 0.27	Capital and CAMELS ratios.
Micronesia	U.S. system.	U.S. system.	Deposits.	Risk-based: 0.00 to 0.27	Capital and CAMELS ratios.
Philippines	...	22 billion pesos.	Deposits.	0.2	
Sri Lanka	...	Very low (80 mil. Rupees).	Deposits.	0.15	
Taiwan Province of China	<5% of insured deposits.	0.3% insured deposits.	Covered deposits.	Risk-based: 0.05 to 0.06 (since 1/1/2000).	9 categories reflecting CAR and rating on the early warning system.
EUROPE					
Austria	...	...	Covered deposits.	pro rata, ex post.	
Belgium	0.5% of insured deposits.	15.8 billion Belgian francs or 0.25% insured deposits.	Covered deposits.	0.02 + 0.04 if necessary.[3]	
Bulgaria	Yes, 5% of total deposits.	30 million new BGL.	Insurable deposits.	0.5[4]	
Croatia	5% of insured deposits.	0.85% of insured deposits end 1998.	Insured deposits.	0.2 can be risk-adjusted.	As determined by the at central bank.
Czech Republic	...	...	Insured deposits.	Commercial banks: 0.5 Savings banks: 0.1	
Denmark	Yes, DKK 3 billion.	...	Allocated as a % of covered deposits.	0.2 (max) of total deposits.	
Estonia	3% of insured deposits.	New scheme.	Deposits until 2002.	0.5% (max).	
Finland	2% of insured deposits.	FIM 300 mil, or 0.14% of insured deposits.	Insured deposits.	Risk-based: 0.05 to 0.3, which can be increased in an emergency.	Solvency ratio.
France	...	New scheme.	Deposits plus ⅓ loans.	Risk-based since June 1999. Previously on demand.	BS calculates the adjustment based on CAMEL-like ratings.
Germany	Yes, 3% of loans.	Target met.	Amount owed to customers.	0.008 in the statutory scheme 0.0 to 0.1 in the private sector.[5]	Risk category and length of membership in the private deposit insurance system.
Gibraltar	No.	New scheme.	Insured deposits.	There is a small fund for administrative expenses; otherwise charges are ex post.	
Greece	A reasonable level.	GD 81 billion at end 1999.	Deposits.[6]	Decreasing by size: .0025 to .125[6] Can be tripled in an emergency.	
Hungary	Informally 1.5% insured deposits.	1% of insured deposits.	Insurable deposits.	0.19, decreasing by size to 0.16 plus risk adjustment.	Additional charge if bank falls below minimum CAR.
Iceland	...	...	Insured deposits.	0.15	

Table A4 (continued)

Region, Country, or Province	Fund Target as a Percent of Deposits	Actual Fund as a Percent of Deposits	Premium or Assessment Base	Annual Premium as a Percentage of the Assessment Base	Basis for Risk-Adjusting Premiums[1]
Ireland	...	...	EU and EEA, i.e., insured deposits at all branches of credit institutions in the EEA.	0.2 at start. Currently no regular premium only extraordinary assessments.	
Italy	0.4–0.8% of covered deposits: for administrative expenses.	0.4% of total deposits.	Protected funds adjusted for size and risk.	Risk-adjusted charges are levied ex post to restore the funds to their required levels.	Index with 28 gradations based on risk, solvency, maturity transformation, and performance.
Latvia	Not specified.	New scheme.	Insured deposits.	0.3	
Lithuania	For savings bank scheme.	100 million Lita or 2.5% of deposits.	Insured deposits.	1.5 falling to 1.0 in 2000.	
Luxembourg	...	...	Insured deposits.	Ex post to a maximum of 5% of capital.	
Macedonia	5% of insured deposits.[7]	3% of insured deposits.	Insured deposits.	Risk-based: 1% to 2..5% plus supplement, if needed.	Capital ratio and financial standing.
Netherlands	...	...	Case by case[8] Share of insured deposits.	Ex post to a maximum of 10% of capital.	
Norway	1.5% deposits + 0.5% risk-adjusted assets.	...	Risk-weighted assets and total deposits.	0.5 of risk-weighted assets 0.15 deposits.	Risk-weighted assets.
Poland	0.4 percent of deposits	1.8 % of insured deposits.	Deposits, also risk-adjusted assets.[9]	not more than 0.4, but includes risk-adjustment.	Risk-weighted assets.
Portugal	...	...	Insured deposits.	Risk-based from 0.08 to 0.12 + more in emergencies.	Condition, including solvency.
Romania	10% of personal deposits.	1.8% of insured deposits.	Insured deposits.	Risk-based from 0.3 to 0.6.	Complex formula reflecting, capital, NPLs, profits, liquidity, and risk assets.
Slovak Republic	1.5% of insured deposits.	0.47% insured deposits.	Insured deposits.	0.1 to 0.3 for banks.[10]	
Spain	1% of deposits.		Insured deposits.	0.1 (Max. of 0.2)	
Sweden	2.5% of total deposits.	...	Covered deposits.	Risk-based, 0.5 now, 0.1 later.	From 60% to 140% of base depending on CAR.
Switzerland	...	...	Discretion but considering gross earnings and balance sheet items, including covered deposits.	Ex post, on demand, varies.	Based on earnings and some discretion.
Turkey	No.	5% of insured deposits.	Insured savings deposits.	Risk-based, 1.0 or 1.2	CAR: banks with more than 8% capital pay the lower rate.
Ukraine	... .	10% insured deposits.	Total deposits.	0.5 plus special charges that are NOT risk-based.	
United Kingdom	£5m–£6m for administrative expenses.	<£3m	EEA deposits i.e., insured deposits.	On demand. Not to exceed 0.3 % of guaranteed deposits.	
MIDDLE EAST					
Bahrain	...	...	Deposits.	ex post.	
Lebanon	...	...	Credit accounts.	0.05[11]	
Morocco	No.	...	Total deposits.	0.2	
Oman	...	...	Deposits.	0.02, but can range from 0.1 to 0.3 over time.	
WESTERN HEMISPHERE					
Argentina	5% of total deposits.	0.1% of total deposits in December 1998.	Insurable deposits.	0.3 basic plus risk adjustment with range from 0.36 to 0.72.	Formula that includes provisions, CAR, CAMEL, and risk assets.
Bahamas	No.	Very new scheme.	Either insured or insurable deposits.	0.05	

Table A4 (continued)

Region, Country, or Province	Fund Target as a Percent of Deposits	Actual Fund as a Percent of Deposits	Premium or Assessment Base	Annual Premium as a Percentage of the Assessment Base	Basis for Risk-Adjusting Premiums[1]
Brazil	5% of guaranteed deposits.	...	Total deposits.	0.3 + 0.15 as an extraordinary contribution.	
Canada	No.	C$500m ~0.19%	Covered deposits.	Risk-adjusted, 0.04 to 0.33.	A complex formula with quantitative and qualitative factors including: capital adequacy, profitability, asset concentration, regulatory rating and adherence to standards.
Chile	No.	...	Not applicable.	None.[12]	
Colombia	...	11.7% of insured deposits at end 1998.[13]	Insured deposits.	0.3, to become risk-adjusted in the year 2000.[14]	A premium refund, based on a rating by an independent rating agency, is pending.
Dominican Republic	...		Deposits.	0.1875	
Ecuador	50% of insured deposits.		Deposits.	0.65+ risk adjustment in the year 2000.	Risk rating to be developed by deposit insurance agency.
El Salvador			Deposits.	0.1. Can be raised to 0.3 to repay debt. Also there is a 50% risk-based mark-up.	If the bank has sub-standard securities or is subject to intervention or special supervision.
Guatemala	10% of covered deposits.	New scheme.	Covered deposits.	1.0 + 0.5 when the fund falls below its target.	
Honduras	5% of deposits.	New scheme.	Deposits.	Not more than 0.25.	
Jamaica	Not de jure: but there is an admin target of 1% of insured deposits.	New scheme J$44.4 million in March 1999.	Insurable deposits.	0.1	
Mexico	No.	0.11% of deposits in March 1998.	Deposits and other liabilities .	0.4 plus special and risk adjustment to 0.8.	As determined by the ministry of finance.
Peru	...	...	Covered deposits.	Base of 0.65 plus risk adjustment.[15]	Risk category as determined by the supervisor.
Trinidad and Tobago	No	TT$ 250 million in 1998.	Deposits.	0.2	
United States	By law: 1.25% of insured deposits.	1.4% of insured deposits.	Domestic deposits.	Risk-based; 0.00 to 0.27.	Capital and CAMELS ratios.[16]
Venezuela	...	4% of total deposits.[17]	Insurable deposits.	2.0[18]	
67 countries*	29 systems have a target, which ranges from 0.4% to 50% of insured deposits.	Resources range from a deficit to 10% of insured deposits.	All deposits: 27, Insured deposits: 36, including Covered deposits: 8, Non-deposit base: 2.	58 countries regularly levy premiums that range from 0.00% to 2.0%, 24 countries risk-adjust their charges.	Varies from the relatively simple compilation of risk-based assets to complex formulae for assessing risk..

Sources: Country authorities; and IMF staff.

Notes: . . . Means data not available.

*Excluding the six African countries whose deposit insurance system agreement is not fully ratified, and Panama, which has explicit coverage only for credit cooperatives.

[1]CAR stands for the capital adequacy ratio. NPLs are non-performing loans. CAMELS stands for capital adequacy, asset quality, management capacity, earnings, liquidity, and systemic risk.

[2] The target in Tanzania is to be raised to this level by June 30, 2001.

[3]The premium in Belgium can be raised by a maximum of 0.04 percent when the funds' liquid assets fall below a critical level.

[4]The Bulgarian fund can request an advance premium of 1.5 percent of the deposit base if it has insufficient resources.

[5]The premium charged by the private deposit insurance schemes in Germany vary by scheme from 0.004 percent to 0.1 percent.

Table A4 *(concluded)*

[6]When the fund reaches a reasonable level in Greece, a bank's premium is based on the increase in its deposits. The deposit insurance system invests 80% of a bank's contribution in a time deposit at the bank.

[7]The target in Macedonia is set at 5% and 15% of deposits in different places in the legislation.

[8]In the Netherlands, the ex post assessments are made case-by-case on the basis of several items of data recently reported to the central bank. A comparison is made between the portfolios of the failed bank and the assessed bank. Costs are apportioned after consultation with the bankers' committee.

[9]Article 25 of the deposit insurance law in Poland sets premiums at no more than 0.4 percent of deposits. However, Article 13 states that premiums should not exceed 0.4 percent of the sum of assets rated according to risk. Banks in Poland keep control over their contributions until they are needed, invest in Treasury securities and keep the interest.

[10]Building societies in the Slovak Republic pay premiums at half the commercial banks' rate. Coverage is adjusted periodically.

[11]In Lebanon, the premium paid by the banks is matched by a contribution from the government.

[12]To reduce central bank exposure, Chilean banks with demand deposits in excess of 2.5 times capital and reserves have to maintain a 100 percent marginal reserve requirement invested in short-term central bank or government securities that are liened to the central bank. The Chilean authorities regard the interest cost of maintaining the reserve requirement as imposing an implicit charge for deposit insurance coverage. The Chilean Central Bank guarantees demand deposits in full. Household savings and time deposits are co-insured 90% by the government to UF 120 (about $3,675) per person per year.

[13]As many of the assets of the insurance fund in Colombia have been lent to weak institutions, the value of the fund's reserves is overstated.

[14]Premiums in Columbia will become risk-based when a risk-rating agency is established in Colombia, hopefully in the year 2000.

[15]The premium in Peru is computed to the maximum amount insured and applies only to deposits of individuals and nonprofit institutions. Banks pay 0.65 percent of total deposits plus 0.2 percent for each higher risk category.

[16]The U.S. is studying the possibility of revising its process of estimating the risk-adjustment.

[17]The fund, FOGADE, has deferred recognizing the losses it suffered during the 1994–95 banking crisis. Consequently, fund reserves are overstated.

[18]Venezuela raised the premium from 0.5 percent to 2.0 percent early in 1994 to help fund the heavy assistance to troubled banks.

Table A5. Deposit Coverage in Explicit Limited Deposit Insurance Systems

Region, Country or Province	Limited Coverage: Measured in Euros and/or U.S. dollars[1]	Per Depositor	Full Coverage	Coinsurance	Offsetting[2]
AFRICA					
Kenya	$1,390	X			Yes.
Nigeria	$140 at the market exchange rate, but $2,430 at the official exchange rate.[3]	X			Yes.
Tanzania	$310	X			Yes.
Uganda	$1,890	X			Yes.
ASIA					
Bangladesh	$2,020	X			Yes.
India	$2,300	X			Yes.
Japan	No, initially $71,000, but in full until April 2002.[4]	X	Yes: until April 2002.		Yes.
Kazakhstan	$1,420 in full, then coinsurance on a sliding scale to $7,110.	X		Yes: above the basic limit.	Yes.
Korea	No: initially $14,600, but in full until the year-end 2000.	X	Yes: until end 2000.		Yes.
Marshall Islands	$100,000	X			Yes.
Micronesia	$100,000	X			Yes.
Philippines	$2,490	X			Yes.
Sri Lanka	$1,330	X			Yes.
Taiwan Province of China	$31,500	X			Yes.
EUROPE					
Austria	€20,000 ($20,900), but coinsurance for businesses.	X		Yes: throughout for businesses.	Yes.
Belgium	€20,000 ($20,900) in year 2000.	X			Yes.
Bulgaria	95% of $1,070n, then 80% to $2,670.	X		Yes, throughout on a two tier scale.	Yes.
Croatia	$13,700 since July 1999.	X		Not since July1999.	...
Czech Republic	90% coinsurance to $11,620.	X		Yes: on all covered accounts.	Yes.
Denmark	€40,250 ($42,325).	X			Yes.
Estonia	Co-insure 90% of $1,210, but €20,000 in 2010.	X		Yes: on all covered accounts.	Yes.
Finland	$27,270	X			Yes.
France	$66,670	X			No.
Germany	The official scheme offers 90% coinsurance to €20,000 ($20,900), but the deductible is covered privately. The private scheme offers coverage to 30% of the bank's capital.[5]	X		Yes: on all publicly insured accounts, but the private deposit insurance system covers the 10% deductible.	Yes.
Gibraltar	Lesser of 90% coinsurance or €20,000 ($20,900).	X		Yes: on all insured accounts.	Yes.
Greece	€20,000 ($20,900)	X			Yes.
Hungary	€4,165 ($4,350)	X			Yes.
Iceland	€20,000 ($20,900)[6]	X			No.
Ireland	Co-insure 90% to €20,000 ($20,900) in 2000.	X	X	Yes: on all insured accounts.	Yes .
Italy	€103,000 ($108,000)	X		Yes.	Yes.
Latvia	$870[7]	X			No.[8]

Table A5 *(continued)*

Region, Country or Province	Limited Coverage: Measured in Euros and/or U.S. dollars[1]	Per Depositor	Full Coverage	Coinsurance	Offsetting[2]
Lithuania	$2,500 in full then coinsurance to $11,250.	X		Yes: above the basic coverage.	Yes.
Luxembourg	Co-insure 90% to €15,000 ($ 15,670) through 1999, then to 90% of €20,000 ($20.900).	X		Yes: on all insured accounts.	No.
Macedonia	Co-insure 75% to DM 10,000 ($5,550).	X		Yes: on all insured accounts.	Yes.
Netherlands	€20,000 ($20,900).	X			Yes.
Norway	$253,520.	X			Yes.
Poland	€1,000 ($1,050) paid in zlotys, then 90% coinsurance for the next €4,000 ($4,180) in 1999, €11,000 ($11,500) in 2000, rising to €20,000 in 2003.	X		Yes: above the basic coverage.	Yes.
Portugal	€15,000 or $15,670, coinsurance to €45,000 ($47,000), through 1999, the €20,000 ($20,900) in 2000.	X		Yes: above the basic coverage.	No.
Romania	$1,920[9]	X			...
Slovak Republic	$6,790[10]	X			Yes.
Spain	€15,000 ($15,670) through 1999, Then €20,000 ($20,900).	X			No.
Sweden	€28,663 ($30,370)[11]	X			Yes.
Switzerland	$19,600	X			Yes.
Turkey	Normally in full only on household accounts.[12]	X	Temporarily in full on all accounts.		No.
Ukraine	$120[13]	X			...
United Kingdom	Larger of 90% coinsurance to $33,333 or €22,222.	X		Yes: on all insured accounts.	Yes.
MIDDLE EAST					
Bahrain	Coinsurance to $5,640.[14]	X		Yes: on all insured accounts.	No.
Lebanon	$3,320	X			No.
Morocco	$5,090	X			Yes.
Oman	$52,080 or 75% coinsurance, whichever is less.	X		Yes: on larger accounts.	Yes.
WESTERN HEMISPHERE					
Argentina	$30,000	X			No.
Bahamas	$50,000	X			Yes.
Brazil	$17,070 (real 20,000)	X			No.
Canada	$40,790[15]	X			Yes.
Chile	Demand deposits in full and 90% coinsurance to UF 120 or $3,400 for savings deposits.[16]	X for total savings deposits in the system.	Only for demand deposits.	On all savings deposits.	No.
Colombia	Co-insure 75% of 10 million pesos ($7,500) and $7,500 flat on larger deposits.	X		On all insured accounts .	No.
Dominican Republic	Coinsurance to $12,280.	Per deposit.		On all insured accounts.	Yes, in 1999 law.
Ecuador	UVC 500 or $3,250.	X			Yes.
El Salvador	$6,280 (indexed to the CPI).	X			Yes.
Guatemala	$2,800[17]	X			Yes, if collateral or matured.

Table A5 *(continued)*

Region, Country or Province	Limited Coverage: Measured in Euros and/or U.S. dollars[1]	Per Depositor	Full Coverage	Coinsurance	Offsetting[2]
Honduras	$7,000	X	Until 2002.		Yes.
Jamaica	$5,000	X	X: until banking system has recovered.		Yes, if in arrears.
Mexico	In full, except subordinated debt, 400,000 UDIs ($90,000) in 2000.[18]	X	Yes: being phased out.		No.
Peru	$17,770	X			Yes.
Trinidad and Tobago	$8,000	X			Yes, on past due loans.
United States	$100,000[19]	X			Yes.
Venezuela	$1,580 according to the law, but payment has been 4 times higher at $6,330.[20]	X			No.
Number of Countries: 67*	67 Countries have explicitly limited coverage in normal times:	66 provide coverage per depositor; only 1 offers covers per deposit.	Full coverage is explicit in 7 of these countries.	20 countries co-insure. 15 impose a haircut on all deposits while 5 co-insure above the basic coverage limit.	Yes: 49 No: 15 … : 3

Sources: Country authorities; and IMF staff.

Notes: . . . Means data are not available.

*Totals exclude six African countries that have agreed upon a regional deposit insurance system, but have yet to ratify the agreement and Panama, which has explicit coverage only for credit cooperatives.

[1]Exchange rates are those at the end of October, 1999.

[2]Offsetting refers to the practice of deducting the value of a depositor's loans or other debts to the bank from his/her insured deposit. Some countries offset (set off, net) the value of all loans from deposits, other set off only past due loans. Yet other countries, such as Argentina, Bahrain, Belgium, France, and Luxembourg that do not offset in general, deduct the value of demand deposits from the value of loans owed.

[3]Coverage in Nigeria is much higher at the official exchange rate than at the market rate.

[4]Japan extended full coverage as an emergency measure and postponed removal from April 2001 until April 2002 in January 2000.

[5]Coverage of the public scheme for commercial banks in Germany is limited to 90 percent and €20,000, but private insurance schemes cover the 10% haircut and cover deposits above the coverage limit. The private schemes for savings banks and credit cooperatives protect deposits by securing the solvency of the institutions as a whole.

[6]Coverage in Iceland in principle is full. The minimum is €20,000. Above that, payment is in proportion to the resources of the fund.

[7]Coverage in Latvia will rise gradually to €20,000 by the year 2008.

[8]The deposit insurance system in Latvia offsets a deposit that is held as collateral for a loan.

[9]The coverage limit in Romania is adjusted each year for inflation.

[10]Coverage in the Slovak Republic is adjusted periodically.

[11]Sweden provided full coverage during the banking crisis in 1992 and withdrew it in 1996.

[12]Turkey has implicitly provided unlimited coverage since May 1994. The full guarantee was made explicit in late 1999.

[13]Coverage in the Ukraine will rise as deposit totals trend upwards.

[14]Bahrain covers the lesser of 75 percent of a deposit or $5,610, as long as the fund's total outlays in any year do not exceed US$9.4 million. In this situation, coverage is determined on a pro rata basis.

[15]Coverage in Canada is extended separately for retirement accounts and deposits held in trust, which are each additionally insured to Can$60,000.

[16]The Chilean Central Bank guarantees demand deposits in full. Household savings and time deposits are co-insured 90% by the government to UF 120 (about $3,400) per person per year.

[17]The coverage limit on Guatemala can be adjusted periodically to cover between 90% and 95% of the number of accounts.

[18]Before the legislation passed in 1998, each December in Mexico, FOBAPROA announced which commercial bank obligations it would protect. Coverage is now comprehensive, but there is a legislative proposal to limit coverage in the year 2005 to UDI 400,000 or approximately $96,000, where UDI are inflation-adjusted units of Mexican currency.

[19]In the United States, separate, additional coverage is offered for retirement and joint accounts.

[20]In 1994, Venezuela selectively paid more than the legally stated limit on coverage.

Table A6. Types of Deposit Covered and Excluded in Countries with Limited Explicit Deposit Insurance Systems

Region, Country or Province	Types of Deposits Covered	Excludes						Household Deposits Only[3]
		Foreign currency deposits[1]	Inter-bank deposits	Government deposits	Insider deposits	Illegal deposits[2]	High-rate deposits	
AFRICA								
Kenya	All							
Nigeria	Most[4]	X			X			
Tanzania	Most	X	X					
Uganda	Most	X	X					
ASIA								
Bangladesh	[5]	X	X	X				X
India	[6]		X	X		X		
Japan	Normally most[7]	Normally X[7]	Normally X[7]	Normally X		Normally X		
Kazakhstan	Only time deposits[8]		X	X	X			X
Korea	Now all: usually most[9]	Normally X[9]	Normally X[9]	Normally X				
Marshall Is.	All[10]							
Micronesia	All							
Philippines	All							
Sri Lanka	[11]	X	X	X				
Taiwan Province of China	[12]	X	X	X				
EUROPE								
Austria	[13]	**	X	X	X	X		[13]
Belgium	[14]	**	X	X			X	X[14]
Bulgaria	[15]		X	X	X		X	X
Croatia	Savings deposits	[16]	X	X	X			X
Czech Republic		X	X		X	X		Widened in 1998
Denmark	Most		X		X	X		
Estonia	[17]		X	X	X	X	X	
Finland	[18]		X	Central government	X	X		
France	[19]	** (paid in francs)	X	Central government				
Germany	[20]	***20	X20	X20	X20	X	X	
Gibraltar	Most	*** Paid in sterling	...					
Greece	[21]		X	Central government	X	X		
Hungary	[22]		X	X	X	X	X	
Iceland	Most[23]		X			X		
Ireland	[24]	***	X		X	X		
Italy	[25]		X	X	X	X		
Latvia	[26]	Paid in local currency	X	X	X			X
Lithuania	[27]	***	X	X	X	X		X

Table A6 (continued)

Region, Country or Province	Types of Deposits Covered	Excludes						Household Deposits Only[3]
		Foreign currency deposits[1]	Inter-bank deposits	Government deposits	Insider deposits	Illegal deposits[2]	High-rate deposits	
Luxembourg	Most		X					
Macedonia	28		X	X				X
Netherlands	29		X					X[29]
Norway	Most[30]		X					
Poland	31	X	X	Central government	X			
Portugal	32	Paid in local currency	X	X	X	X	32	
Romania	33		X	X	X			X
Slovak Republic	34		X	X	X			X
Spain	35		X	X	X			
Sweden	Most[36]		X					
Switzerland	Savings deposits	X	X	X				X
Turkey	37		Normally X	Normally X				Normally X
Ukraine	38	X	X	X	X	X	X	X
United Kingdom	Most[39]	*** paid in sterling	X		X	X		
MIDDLE EAST								
Bahrain	40		X	X	X	X		
Lebanon	Most[41]	X[41]			X			
Morocco	All[42]							
Oman	Most[43]	Paid in local currency	X		X	X		
WESTERN HEMISPHERE								
Argentina	Most[44]		X				X	
Bahamas	All[45]							
Bolivia	Most		X		X			
Brazil	Most[46]		X		X			
Canada	Most[47]	X						
Chile	48		X					X for savings and time deposits[48]
Colombia	Most	X			X			
Dominican Republic	Savings and time deposits in savings associations[49]		X					
Ecuador	50				Normally X		X	Normally X
El Salvador	Most[51]		X		X	X		
Guatemala	Savings deposits only[52]	X						
Honduras	53	Paid in local currency	X	X	X	X	X	
Jamaica	Most[54]	Paid in local currency	X					
Mexico	All[55]		X (normally)		X	X		

Table A6 *(continued)*

Region, Country or Province	Types of Deposits Covered	Excludes						Household Deposits Only[3]
		Foreign currency deposits[1]	Inter-bank deposits	Government deposits	Insider deposits	Illegal deposits[2]	High-rate deposits	
Peru	All demand deposits[56]		X	X	X	X		X (All deposits for natural persons and non profits)
Trinidad & Tobago	Most[57]	X	X					
United States	All domestic[58]							
Venezuela	Most	X	X					
Number of Countries: 67*	8 countries cover all types of deposit; 21 cover most types.	26 countries exclude foreign exchangedeposits: 17 countries exclude all; 9 exclude some foreign exchange deposits.	54 countries normally exclude inter-bank deposits.	33 countries exclude some or all government deposits.	34 countries exclude insider deposits.	23 countries explicitly exclude illegal deposits.	9 countries exclude deposits carrying very high rates.	18 countries cover only or mainly household deposits.

Sources: Country authorities; and IMF staff.

Notes: . . . Information is not available.

*Totals exclude six African countries that have agreed upon a regional deposit insurance system, but have yet to ratify the agreement and Panama.

**Indicates coverage is extended to deposits in the domestic currency, euros, or the currencies of other members of the EU.

***Indicates coverage is extended to deposits in sterling, euros, or the currencies of other members of the European Economic Area (which includes the EU).

[1]Deposits that are denominated in a foreign currency.

[2]Frequently refers to deposits that are money-laundered.

[3]Indicates that only individual or household deposits are covered. Sometimes the deposits of small businesses or not-for-profit organizations are also covered.

[4]All domestic-currency deposits in licensed banks in Nigeria are covered except those of directors and staff, as well as deposits that serve as collateral for a loan.

[5]Bangladesh does not insure the deposits of domestic and foreign governments, or financial institution or inter-bank deposits.

[6]India insures deposits in commercial, cooperative, and rural banks, except certificates of deposits, government, inter-bank, and illegal deposits.

[7]Japan has two deposit insurance systems. The first covers commercial and shinkin banks, and labor and credit associations. It normally insures demand and time deposits in domestic currency, including installment savings and money in trust whose principal has been guaranteed. However, the authorities have extended a temporary full guarantee. The second scheme covers agricultural and fishery cooperatives.

[8]Kazakhstan excludes bearer deposits, trust accounts, deposits of individuals engaged in entrepreneurial activity, and insider deposits from coverage.

[9]Korea has placed a temporary full guarantee on deposits.

[10]Two U.S. banks are insured by the FDIC, but the domestic bank is not covered.

[11]Sri Lanka excludes government, public corporation, and other banks' deposits from coverage.

[12]Taiwan Province of China excludes negotiable CDs, the deposits of governments at all levels and those of financial institutions.

[13]Austria excludes government, large corporation, insider and criminal deposits, but insures the deposits of natural persons in full, up to the coverage limit, while coverage for other non-household deposits is limited to 90 percent of the guaranteed deposit.

[14]Belgium covers the deposits, bank notes, bonds and other claims on banks of households, and small and medium-sized non-financial enterprises.

[15]Bulgaria excludes insider deposits and those paying preferential interest rates.

[16]Croatia excludes foreign currency deposits placed prior to 1993 as they were covered by an issuance of government bonds.

[17]Estonia excludes the deposits of insiders, money-launderers, governments at all levels, larger businesses, financial institutions, including insurance companies, other members of the same corporate group, and those that pay substantially higher rates.

[18]In its new system that replaces its comprehensive guarantee, Finland excludes the deposits of the central government and credit institutions.

[19]France has separate schemes for commercial banks and for mutual, savings and cooperative banks. Coverage excludes deposits of the central government, insiders, affiliated enterprises, and money-launderers' deposits, together with the debt securities issued by the insured institution.

[20]The statutory scheme in Germany insures all deposits except inter-bank, government, institutional investor, and insider deposits and those that receive exceptionally high interest rates. There are separate private schemes for commercial banks, savings banks, giro institutions, and credit cooperatives. The Deposit Protection Fund established by the Association of German Bankers covers the deposits of non-bank creditors (both resident and non-resident) that are held in Germany and abroad, regardless of currency denomination. It includes insider accounts.

[21]Greece excludes inter-bank, insider, central government, and illegal deposits and negotiable CDs, acceptances, promissory notes and repurchase agreements.

[22]Hungary insures registered deposits but excludes the deposits of the government, insiders, professional investors, and money launderers.

[23]Iceland covers all liabilities, except inter-bank and money-laundered deposits, accounts of subsidiaries and parent companies and bonds, bankers' drafts, and other claims issued by the insured institution in the form of transferable securities.

[24]Ireland does not insure certificates of deposit, the deposits of major owners and senior managers, governments at all levels, large corporations, or those involved in money laundering.

Table A6 *(concluded)*

[25]Italy insures all deposits except bearer deposits, criminal, government, insider, and inter-bank deposits under two separate deposit insurance systems, one for banks and the other for cooperative institutions.

[26]The deposit insurance law in Latvia was enacted in May 1998 and came into effect on October 1, 1998. It does not cover insider deposits or accounts in banks already declared bankrupt or insolvent or that have already entered liquidation proceedings.

[27]The deposit protection scheme in Lithuania excludes anonymous, illegal, and insider deposits and interest.

[28]Macedonia guarantees the current account and savings deposits of resident natural persons that are denominated in dinars and foreign currencies.

[29]The Netherlands excludes the deposits of large corporations, other banks, insurance companies, and insiders, but covers those of small enterprises and small foundations, in addition to those of households.

[30]Norway has two separate deposit insurance funds-one for commercial banks and the other for savings banks. Deposits by all financial institutions and other companies in the same group as the member are excluded.

[31]Poland does not guarantee the deposits of a bank's significant stockholders, its directors, or senior mangers, the deposits of the Treasury, investment firms, or insurance companies. The National Savings Bank-a State Bank, the Polish Guardian Bank, the Food Management Bank and cooperative banks, whose deposits continue to be insured in full by the Treasury through 1999, would, however, pay out at most 0.2 percent of insured deposits. The Treasury also insures some household savings deposits.

[32]Portugal guarantees demand, time, and foreign currency deposits, but not those of insiders or criminals, financial institutions, or central and local governments. The Portuguese law states that "deposits for which the depositor has, on an individual basis, unjustifiably obtained loans from the same credit institution, rate or other financial concessions, which have helped to aggravate its financial situation," shall be excluded.

[33]The deposit insurance system in Romania protects household deposits and excludes inter-bank, government, insider, and illegal deposits from coverage.

[34]The Slovak Republic does not protect inter-bank, government, or anonymous deposits or those of owners, directors and senior managers.

[35]There are three separate deposit insurance systems in Spain: one for commercial banks, a second for savings banks, and the third for credit cooperatives. The deposits of financial institutions, public bodies, and insiders are not covered.

[36]Before its banking crisis, Sweden did not have a system of depositor protection. It introduced a temporary guarantee of all bank liabilities in 1992, and replaced it with a formal system of deposit insurance to conform to EU standards in January 1996 for all banks and investment firms that receive deposits.

[37]Turkey insured savings deposits and CDs denominated in Turkish lira, and also the savings accounts of real persons domiciled in Turkey that are denominated in foreign exchange. In December 1999, a guarantee was extended by decree to all deposits.

[38]Ukraine does not cover the deposits of insiders or their families.

[39]The United Kingdom does not cover the deposits of financial institutions.

[40]Bahrain ensures all deposits held in the Bahraini offices of full commercial banks, except government, illegal, and inter-bank deposits, and those held by affiliates, shareholders, directors and officers of the bank.

[41]Lebanon ensures all deposits denominated in Lebanese pounds, except those of senior insiders, and auditors. Under a transitory law passed in 1991, which initially was due to expire at end 1998, deposits denominated in foreign currency are also insured.

[42]Oman excludes deposits of significant shareholders, directors and senior managers, illegal deposits and the deposits of auditors, parent, subsidiary and affiliated companies.

[43]In Morocco, depositors who have committed a serious crime against the failed institutions are not compensated.

[44]In Argentina, inter-bank deposits and deposits that pay more than 200 basis points above the reference rate are not insured.

[45]The Bahamas excludes the deposits of persons who have contributed to the bank's failure from coverage.

[46]Brazil does not insure inter-bank deposits or the deposits of connected parties.

[47]Insured deposits in Canada include: savings and demand deposits; term deposits such as guaranteed investment certificates and debentures issued by loan companies; money orders and drafts and checks; and traveler's checks issued by member institutions if they are denominated in Canadian dollars.

[48]In Chile, the central bank guarantees demand deposits. The government guarantees 90 percent of household savings and time deposits to a limit of UF 120 per person per year, that is, 120 inflation-adjusted units of Chilean currency.

[49]The Dominican Republic has explicit deposit insurance only for savings and loan associations and the National Housing Bank. A provision to give small depositors protection in a wider range of institutions by giving them priority over the assets of a failed bank passed the legislative but was vetoed by the President.

[50]Ecuador's deposit insurance coverage is normally confined to household deposits. It also does not cover the deposits of owners, current or recent directors or managers or deposits that pay more than 3 percent above the average rate. The deposit insurance system covers off-shore deposits.

[51]El Salvador is implementing a new deposit insurance system that covers all deposits, including off-shore deposits, but excluding inter-bank and insider deposits.

[52]Coverage in Guatemala does not extend to accumulated interest.

[53]The deposit insurance system in Honduras (FOSEDE) insures demand, savings, and term deposits held by individuals or corporate entities in national or foreign currency. Deposits of other financial institutions, institutional investors, the public sector, members of the same corporate group, insiders, and those who contributed to the insolvency of the failed bank are not eligible for coverage. Neither are deposits that carry significantly higher rates or are illegal.

[54]The Jamaica Deposit Insurance Corporation pays foreign currency deposits in Jamaican dollars, and does not cover inter-bank deposits.

[55]Under FOBAPROA, Mexico did not explicitly impose an obligation on its insurance agency to guarantee deposits, but each December, the agency announced what instruments it would cover. For example, in 1997, it stated that it would cover all liabilities of commercial banks except subordinated debt. Also excluded were illicit transactions, inter-bank credits through the Bank of Mexico's transfer systems, and obligations of intermediaries that were part of the bank's financial group. Under the new deposit insurance system established in 1998 (IPAB), there are normally new exclusions that are temporarily overridden by the full guarantee.

[56]Peru ensures all types of deposits, except bearer certificates, for natural persons and nonprofit organizations. The deposit insurance system also insures demand deposits for companies and corporations.

[57]Trinidad and Tobago insures demand, savings, and time deposits, but not inter-bank or foreign currency deposits, or those of affiliated companies.

[58]Deposit insurance in the United States is compulsory for nationally chartered and for almost all state-chartered banks and thrifts. Deposits booked off-shore are not covered.

Table A7. Effective Coverage in Selected Countries

Region, Country, or Province[1]	Percentage of the Number of Deposit Accounts Covered	Percentage of the Value of Deposits Covered[2]	Time to Payment
AFRICA			
Kenya	83.3	16	...
Nigeria	78	21	Depositors have 18 months to file claims. By law, compensation is paid only when the assets of the failed bank are sold or loans repaid.
Tanzania	54	12	...
Uganda	95	26	...
ASIA			
Bangladesh	96	31	5 months
India	98	72	...
Japan	100	Normally 78.8 of deposits, now 100	Advance payment for immediate living expenses in one week.
Korea	100	In full	2 months to create eligible list, plus one month to pay.
Philippines			Very slow because of poor deposit records.
Sri Lanka	Negligible	Negligible	Notice within one week, payment within 15 days of claim.
Taiwan Province of China	94	45	...
EUROPE			
Bulgaria		<35	45 days
Croatia	95	68	Starts within 15 days.
Denmark	Probably almost all.	less than 50	...
Estonia	...	1	Starts within 30 days., completed within 3 months.
Finland	96 of the accounts	40	3 months
France	85–90	Low	...
Germany			Within 21 days.
Hungary	97 of the accounts	48 of all deposits 69 of insurable deposits	Starts within 30 days.
Italy	[3]	62[3]	...
Latvia	94.7 of natural persons' accounts	18.7	Set in law.
Lithuania	98.8 of natural persons' accounts	44 of total deposits	...
Macedonia	Virtually all household accounts	99 of deposits are in accounts covered by some insurance	To commence within 45 days of closure.
Norway	99.8	76.1	...
Poland			30 days to create list, 7 days for announcement.
Romania	96	...	...
Slovak Republic	...	47	...
Spain	94[4]	60[5]	...
Turkey	Normally of 100 of real persons' deposits, now all deposits	100	2 weeks in 1994.
Ukraine	...	19	3 months
United Kingdom	70 of claimants	...	Within 3 months of the insolvency, depositor has to claim and the claim be verified.
WESTERN HEMISPHERE			
Argentina	95	40	...
Brazil	955	11 to 12	...
Canada	~85–90	35.9	Between 5 and 50 days in mid 1990s and also makes advance payment.

Table A7. Effective Coverage in Selected Countries

Region, Country, or Province[1]	Percentage of the Number of Deposit Accounts Covered	Percentage of the Value of Deposits Covered[2]	Time to Payment
Chile	94 of time deposits	9 of value of time deposits	...
Columbia	98	34	...
El Salvador			80% is paid within 30 days.
Guatemala	Between 90 and 95 by law.		10 business days.
Jamaica	90	33.5	No provision in the law.
Mexico	Temporarily 100	Temporarily 100	90 days
Trinidad and Tobago	96.3	34.1	To commence within 3 months.
United States	99 of accounts	65.2	Typically within 3 days.
Countries : 41	From negligible to 99, excluding countries offering full coverage.	From negligible to 76, excluding countries offering full coverage.	From 3 days to unspecified. Typically to commence within 3 months.[6]

Notes: ... Means data are not available.

[1]Forty-one countries provided information in response to a special request for data or in published reports.

[2]Countries offset loans (in some cases, all loans, and in other cases, only past-due loans against insured deposits.

[3]The value of deposits covered by insurance declined after Italy lowered its coverage limits.

[4]The percentages of the number of deposits covered by Spain's three schemes are: 94, 94, and 93 percent.

[5]The percentages of the value of deposits covered by Spain's three schemes are: 53, 61, and 63 percent.

[6]Austria, Gibraltar, Greece, Ireland, and Portugal follow EU law by requiring payment to be made within 3 months, unless an exceptional extension of another 3 months is granted. Sweden aims to pay in less than 3 months.

Table A8. Administering the Deposit Insurance System

Region, Country or Province	Govt. Aid[1]	Administration			Formal Relationships	Information Sharing
		Private	Joint	Government/ public[2]		
AFRICA						
Kenya	X			X	Independent de jure, but in practice is an integral part of the central bank. The deposit insurer works closely with the banking supervisor.	Yes, the deposit insurance agency receives on-and off-site reports.
Nigeria	X			X	The independent deposit insurance agency corporation has a harmonious relationship with the ministry of finance, which (together with the central bank) supervises it. The central bank is also the banking supervisor. The 5-member board is appointed by the President of Nigeria and includes the governor of the central bank, the ministry of finance, plus the deposit insurance agency's Managing and two Executive Directors.	Yes, cooperation is good. The NDIC conducts on- and off-site supervisor.
Tanzania	X	X			The independent deposit insurance agency depends on the examination reports of the central bank, which acts also as the banking supervisor.	Yes: From the central bank/banking supervisor.
Uganda	X			X	No separate deposit insurance agency; the deposit insurance system is the responsibility of central bank, which is also banking supervisor	Yes
ASIA						
Bangladesh	X			X	The deposit insurance system is a separate legal entity, but is a part of the central bank, has the same board, and its finances are currently commingled.	Data for a deposit payout comes from the liquidator.
India	X			X	The deposit insurance agency is a wholly owned subsidiary of central bank, of which banking supervisor is a also a part. There are NO supervisors on the deposit insurance system board.	The deposit insurer has access to bank records by law: depends on the banking supervisor for exam reports. Needs improvement.
Japan	X			X	The deposit insurance system is supervised by the Financial Rehabilitation Committee (FRC) and the ministry of finance.	Yes, by law, but it is problematic in practice.
Kazakhstan	X		X		The deposit insurance system is a separate legal entity. The central bank appoints 3 of 9 directors and the ministry of finance appoints one other.	Yes: on condition and deposits by agreement with the central bank and from members.
Korea	X			X	The KDIC reports to the ministry of finance and is separate from the central bank and the FSA (the banking supervisor). The 9-member board has 2 government appointees, a banker, and 4 representatives of financial institutions.	The KDIC collects the data it needs on deposits and bank condition. Also, the deposit insurance agency can require the banking supervisor to examine member banks.
Marshall Is.				X	As in the United States.	As in the United States.
Micronesia				X	There is no relationship between the local supervisors and the FDIC in the United States, which insures the banks.	There are no arrangements for sharing information.
Philippines	X			X	The PDIC is a separate, independent agency.	Hampered by a deposit secrecy law. Relies on the central bank and banking supervisor for exam reports.
Sri Lanka	X			X	The deposit insurance system is administered by the supervisor department of the central bank	Yes: no problems were reported.
Taiwan Province of China	X			X	The deposit insurance agency was established by the ministry of finance, but its role has grown subsequently. It has, for example, taken over responsibility for examining institutions from the ministry of finance.	Yes: the deposit insurance agency is the banking supervisor and conducts bank examinations.

Table A8 *(continued)*

Region, Country or Province	Govt. Aid[1]	Administration			Formal Relationships	Information Sharing
		Private	Joint	Government/ public[2]		
EUROPE						
Austria	X	X			The deposit insurance agency is a private company.	
Belgium	X		X		The deposit insurance system is a responsibility of a separate banking supervisor that may be transferred to the central bank.	Yes: sharing is authorized.
Bulgaria	X		X		The deposit insurance agency is a separate legal entity, but is dependent on the central bank. Of the five-member board, one each comes from the central bank, the goverrnment and the banks, and two are independent.	Yes: but the deposit insurance agency is dependent on the central bank to provide information on condition. The deposit insurance agency can demand information from member banks.
Croatia	X			X[3]	The deposit insurance agency is part of the Bank Restructuring Agency, which is independent de jure. Government officials are members of deposit insurance agency board.	Yes, informally, as needed. Members are required, by law, to provide data to the deposit insurance agency on deposits and condition.
Czech Republic	X			X	The deposit insurance agency is a separate legal entity. Its 5 board members are appointed by the ministry of finance-one from the central bank and 2 from the banks.	No formal agreement to exchange information, but it is obtained from depositors and the central bank.
Denmark	X	X[4]			The private, independent deposit insurance agency is under the supervisor of the banking supervisor (FSA), but is located in the central bank, which provides staff.	Yes; but data come mainly from member banks and auditors.
Estonia	X		X		The deposit insurance agency is a separate legal entity under Public Law. It cooperates with the supervisor. Of its 5-member board, 4 are appointed from the government and there is one banker.	Yes, as required by law, the central bank and member banks provide data. Information for a payout comes from the liquidator.
Finland	X	X			The deposit insurance agency is supervised by the banking supervisor and the ministry of finance; the central bank has no role.	Yes: the government sets the standards for cooperation.
France	No	X			The new deposit insurance system board is private, independent and represents its member institutions. It always has representatives from the 4 largest contributors. The banking supervisor sets the premiums.	Yes, by law but it is difficult in practice. Banking supervisor assesses risks, calculates the risk-adjustment, and passes the data to the deposit insurer.
Germany	…	X (private)	X (official)		The official scheme is part of banking supervisor, which determines what compensation to pay. The ministry of finance approves the by-laws and sets premiums. The Bundesbank is not involved.[5]	The deposit insurance agency can collect info, which it must share with the banking supervisor by law. It is also obliged to consult the banking supervisor.
Gibraltar	No		X		The deposit insurance agency is independent de jure. The Ministry of Industry and Trade appoints the 6-member board from among the banking supervisor, auditors, lawyers, and bankers.	The banks provide data for calculating premiums; depositors and the liquidator for payouts.
Greece	…		X		The deposit insurance agency is a legal entity governed by private law. It is run by the Bankers' Association, which has full decision-making powers, under the budgetary supervisor of the Minister of the Economy. Its 7-member board is appointed by the ministry of finance, the central bank and the Bankers' Association.	Members have to report data regularly. The deposit insurance agency has NO power to inspect banks. Data come from the banking supervisor for premiums (not condition), the failed bank for payouts, and from the home supervisor for foreign branches.

Table A8 *(continued)*

Region, Country or Province	Govt. Aid[1]	Administration			Formal Relationships	Information Sharing
		Private	Joint	Government/ public[2]		
Hungary	X		X		The deposit insurance agency is a legal entity, separate from the banking supervisor and central bank, but the State grants it limited authority. The board is appointed from the ministry of finance, central bank, banking supervisor, the CEO, and the banking industry.	Yes, by formal agreement, with the banking supervisor and from members. However, more information is needed to be commensurate with the increase in the deposit insurance agency's responsibilities.
Iceland	No				The board of the banks' deposit insurance system is appointed by the government. The system is supervised by the banking supervisor.	Data come primarily from the banks and from an informal exchange with the banking supervisor.
Ireland	...			X	The deposit insurance system is run by the central bank.	...
Italy	X	X[6]			The private-consortium deposit insurance system is closely knit with the BOI, which is also the banking supervisor. The BOI approves the deposit insurance system's by-laws.	Yes, by law, but formal notification is required and the issue is sensitive as the deposit insurance system is privately run. The system also obtains data directly from member banks.
Latvia	X			X	The deposit insurance agency, a public institution, is overseen by the ministry of finance: de jure there is a relationship between the deposit insurance agency and the central bank. Four of the five board members are appointed by the government, the fifth comes from the bankers' association.	No, data come from bank reports and depositors' claims.
Lithuania	X			X	The deposit insurance agency, an independent state enterprise, was established by the ministry of finance: Two of its six board members come from the central bank, and two from the ministry of finance, one from the Budget Commission, and the other from the bankers' association.	By law, information is obtained directly from the banks and from the central bank.
Luxembourg	...	X			...	...
Macedonia	X	X			The deposit insurer is a private share-holding company, which is overseen by the central bank. The 7-member Supervisory Board is appointed by the Assembly and includes at least one representative of savings houses and one from the central bank. The Managing Board has three members.	Sharing is said to be inadequate as the deposit insurer is a private company. Data on deposits comes from members and on condition from the central bank.
Netherlands	X			X	The deposit insurance system is run by the central bank.	The deposit insurance system obtains data directly from the banks.
Norway	X	X[7]			The two deposit insurance agencies are separate legal entities, both approved by the ministry of finance. The central bank and banking supervisor are represented on the deposit insurance agency boards.	Yes: the law requires the central bank to provide requested data.
Poland	X		X		The deposit insurance agency is a legal entity under the ministry of finance. Three of the nine board members are appointed by the ministry of finance, three by the central bank, and three by the Bankers' Association.	Yes: by law the central bank must supply the information the deposit insurance agency requests and it also obtains data from banks for its early detection system.
Portugal	X			X	The deposit insurance agency is an autonomous public legal person housed at the central bank and is under ministry of finance direction.	The deposit insurer obtains deposit and condition data directly from member banks. By law, the central bank provides technical and administrative services.

Table A8 (continued)

Region, Country or Province	Govt. Aid[1]	Administration			Formal Relationships	Information Sharing
		Private	Joint	Government/ public[2]		
Romania	X		X		The deposit insurance agency is independent de jure, but the central bank, which is also the banking supervisor, approves its by-laws. Of the 7-member board, three members are appointed by the central bank, and one each by the ministry of justice, the ministry of finance, and the Bankers' Association.	Yes.
Slovak Republic	X		X		The deposit insurance agency is independent de jure, but is supervised by the central bank.	Yes.
Spain	X		X		The deposit insurance agencies have public legal status under the Bank of Spain (the central bank). Of the 8-member board, four members are appointed by the central bank and four by the banks.	Yes
Sweden	X			X	The small deposit insurance agency is under the Bank Support Authority and the ministry of finance: it consults with the banking supervisor and shares its premises.	Yes, but data come primarily from member institutions and the liquidator of a failed bank.
Switzerland	...	X			The deposit insurance system is run by the Swiss Bankers' Association. The Banking Commission is separate from the central bank.	Data are passed from banks to the banking supervisor, which conveys them to the deposit insurance system.
Turkey	X			X	The deposit insurance agency is a judicial entity under the newly independent banking supervisor.	Yes: the deposit insurance agemcy can request the data it needs from the parent banking supervisor.
Ukraine	X			X	The deposit insurance agency is an independent, state-run commercial organization, operated by the central bank. Of its five-member board, two members come from the cabinet, two from the central bank, and one is a banker.	Yes, by law and the deposit insurance agency can inspect banks. It also obtains data from the central bank and from the liquidator for a payout.
United Kingdom	No	[8]		X	The deposit insurance agency acts as a separate legal entity, but is staffed by the banking supervisor (FSA). (The central bank is now responsible only for monetary policy issues.) The board includes, ex officio, the chairman of the FSA, the head of supervisor, the Governor of the central bank and three bankers.	No, information comes from members and auditors; and for a payout, from the liquidator and depositors, who have to apply for payment.
MIDDLE EAST						
Bahrain	...		X		Of the 10-member board, two members come from the central bank, three from various ministries, one from the Chamber of Commerce, and four are commercial bankers, and the final member is the liquidator.	Data for a payout are obtained directly from the depositors of the failed bank.
Lebanon	X		X		The deposit insurer is a cooperative, joint-stock company. Of its seven board members, three come from the government and four from the banks.	There is a bank secrecy law. Depositors submit claims to a court-appointed receivership committee, which conveys the data to the deposit insurance system.
Morocco	No			X	The deposit insurance system is administered by the central bank, which is also the bank supervisor. The ministry of finance promulgates the deposit insurance system's regulations.	Nothing is stipulated in the law, but the banking supervisor and the deposit insurance system are part of the same agency

Table A8 *(continued)*

Region, Country or Province	Govt. Aid[1]	Administration			Formal Relationships	Information Sharing
		Private	Joint	Government/ public[2]		
Oman	X			X	The deposit insurance agency is part of the central bank, but has separate accounts. The central bank can amend any rule governing the deposit insurance system at its discretion.	The central bank, which is also the banking supervisor, has the data it needs to operate the deposit insurance system. It also obtains data from banks.
WESTERN HEMISPHERE						
Argentina	X (small)	X		Central bank input	The deposit insurance agency is a private legal entity that is authorized by central bank, led by central bank representatives, and cooperates with the banking supervisor.	Yes: The deposit insurance system has to request information from the banking supervisor.
Bahamas	X			X	The deposit insurance agency is a separate corporation that is subordinate to the central bank and the ministry of finance.	By law, the deposit insurance system obtains data from member banks.
Brazil	X	X			Insurance is provided by a private, nonprofit company that is supervised by the central bank. All members of the five-member board are bank managers.	The private deposit insurance system has a problem in obtaining data on condition. Data for calculating premiums are supplied by the central bank.
Canada	X			X	The members of the independent deposit insurance system's board include, ex officio, one each from the central bank and ministry of finance and two from the banking supervisor. The deposit insurance agency is accountable to Parliament through the ministry of finance.	Yes: good-facilitated by a Strategic Alliance Agreement between the CDIC and the banking supervisor.
Chile	X			X	There is no separate deposit insurance agency. The central bank covers demand deposits and the ministry of finance protects savings deposits. The deposit insurance system is run by the central bank, which is closely related to the banking supervisor.	Yes, there are significant exchanges of information among the central bank, banking supervisor, and ministry of finance.
Colombia	X			X	The deposit insurance system is owned by the government, run by the central bank, and is under the control of the ministry of finance.	The deposit insurance system plans to rely on information from an independent rating agency.
Dominican Republic	X		X		The deposit insurance system has its own legal personality and capital, but it is subordinate to the banking supervisor. The deposit insurance agency has to seek the approval of the Monetary Board to set premiums and operating rules.	The deposit insurance system obtains information from the banking supervisor.
Ecuador	X			X	The deposit insurance agency is an autonomous, public-law institution under the bank supervisor. The 4-member board includes one representative each from the banking supervisor, ministry of finance, central bank, and the public.	Information is obtained from the banking supervisor.
El Salvador	X			X	The deposit insurer is an autonomous public institution, subject to oversight by the banking supervisor. It consults with the central bank, banking supervisor, and ministry of finance on bank rehabilitiation. Of the five-member board, two members come from the central bank and two from healthy banks.	By law it obtains the information it needs from the central bank and banking supervisor.
Guatemala	X			X	The deposit insurance system is supervised by the banking supervisor. The Bank of Guatemala, the central bank, is the trustee of the deposit insurance system's funds, and represents it before the Monetary Board.	The deposit insurance system obtains data from the banks each month to calculate premiums, and from the banking supervisor when it needs extra funds.

Table A8 (continued)

Region, Country or Province	Govt. Aid[1]	Administration			Formal Relationships	Information Sharing
		Private	Joint	Government/ public[2]		
Honduras	X			X	The deposit insurance system is a decentralized entity under the central bank, but has technical administrative, and budgetary independence. Three members of its five-member board are public officials, two are private including one from the bankers' association.	By law the banking supervisor and central bank are required to provide data requested by FOSEDE, which can also obtain data from member banks.
Jamaica	X			X	The deposit insurance agency is an independent statutory body that cooperates with the central bank, which is also the banking supervisor. It needs the approval of the ministry of finance. Of the seven-member board, three members come ex officio from the government; and four are appointed by the ministry of finance.	Yes, sharing is required by law, but has proved problematic in practice, because the JDIC must request on-site reports from the banking supervisor.
Mexico	X			X	Unlike the old insurer (FOBPROA), the new deposit insurance agency (IPAB) has legal and financial independence. Its seven-member board has a representative from the central bank, ministry of finance and banking supervisor plus four independent members nominated by the Executive and confirmed by the Senate.	Yes, by law but IPAB is dependent on the banking supervisor and the banks for data. It can also conduct examinations.
Peru	X		X		The deposit insurance agency is a private legal entity that is subject to regulation by the banking supervisor. Of its six board members, one member comes from the central bank, one from the banking supervisor, one from the ministry of finance, and the other three are drawn from financial institutions.	The banking supervisor has the necessary information and it makes the payments, after demanding funds from the deposit insurance system.
Trinidad and Tobago	X			X	The deposit insurance agency is a separate, independent legal entity, but the central bank and ministry of finance set the by-laws. It is housed in the central bank.	Yes, but only at the discretion of the central bank.
United States	X			X	The deposit insurance agency is a separate legal entity; it cooperates with the other supervisors, and performs banking supervisor functions for some state-chartered institutions. Of its five-member board, two members are ex officio supervisors, and three represent the public. No more than three can belong to any one political party.	Yes, but disagreements leading to delays have occurred between the different agencies involved. The deposit insurance agency has back-up supervisory authority for those banks it does not supervise, but rarely uses it.
Venezuela	X			X[9]	The deposit insurance agency (FOGADE) is an autonomous legal entity that is supervised of the banking supervisor (and the ministry of finance for administrative purposes). The board has seven members: the chairman and four others are appointed by the President.	By law, the deposit insurance system obtains the examination reports of weak banks and information on deposits to calculate premiums from the banking supervisor.
Number of Countries: 67*	55 countries financially support their system of deposit insurance.	13 Schemes are privately run.	6 Schemes are jointly run.	39 Schemes are run by the government.	29 deposit insurance agencies are independent legal entities: 22 are under central bank; 11 are under the ministry of finance; and 10 are under the separate bank supervisor.	Agencies in 40 countries share information; 13 go directly to banks and the public. Several acknowledge deficiencies in their arrangements.

Sources: Country authorities; and IMF staff.

Notes: ... Means data are not available.

*Excluding the six African countries all of which have not ratified the agreement for a regional system of deposit insurance and Panama.

[1]Reflects situations where the government, which is understood to include the central bank, has provided initial funding, has an obligation to supply loans or guarantees, or has borne losses.

Table A8 *(concluded)*

[2]Is administered by a public body.

[3]In Croatia, the system is administered by a private agency, but some decisions must be approved by the central bank.

[4]In Denmark, the deposit insurance system is privately run although the board is appointed by the government.

[5]The private system of deposit insurance in Germany is run by a commission of 10 persons that represent groups of commercial banks. It has no public oversight. The banking supervisor and private deposit insurance system cooperate.

[6]Although the scheme is privately run in Italy, all decisions must be approved by the central bank so the deposit insurance system has little independent authority.

[7]Norway has two schemes. Both are privately run, but each has two public members of its seven-member board—one from the central bank and the other from the Banking and Securities Commission.

[8]The U.K. Deposit Protection Board is a statutory body established under the Banking Act. The U.K. system has been characterized as privately run, but this is inappropriate.

[9]The seven-member deposit insurance board in Venezuela includes four government appointees, one representative from the banks, one from the labor union, and one from the insurance agency's employees.

Recent Occasional Papers of the International Monetary Fund

197. Deposit Insurance: Actual and Good Practices, by Gillian G.H. Garcia. 2000.

196. Trade and Trade Policies in Eastern and Southern Africa, by a staff team led by Arvind Subramanian, with Enrique Gelbard, Richard Harmsen, Katrin Elborgh-Woytek, and Piroska Nagy. 2000.

195. The Eastern Caribbean Currency Union—Institutions, Performance, and Policy Issues, by Frits van Beek, José Roberto Rosales, Mayra Zermeño, Ruby Randall, and Jorge Shepherd. 2000.

194. Fiscal and Macroeconomic Impact of Privatization, by Jeffrey Davis, Rolando Ossowski, Thomas Richardson, and Steven Barnett. 2000.

193. Exchange Rate Regimes in an Increasingly Integrated World Economy, by Michael Mussa, Paul Masson, Alexander Swoboda, Esteban Jadresic, Paolo Mauro, and Andy Berg. 2000.

192. Macroprudential Indicators of Financial System Soundness, by a staff team led by Owen Evans, Alfredo M. Leone, Mahinder Gill, and Paul Hilbers. 2000.

191. Social Issues in IMF-Supported Programs, by Sanjeev Gupta, Louis Dicks-Mireaux, Ritha Khemani, Calvin McDonald, and Marijn Verhoeven. 2000.

190. Capital Controls: Country Experiences with Their Use and Liberalization, by Akira Ariyoshi, Karl Habermeier, Bernard Laurens, Inci Ötker-Robe, Jorge Iván Canales Kriljenko, and Andrei Kirilenko. 2000.

189. Current Account and External Sustainability in the Baltics, Russia, and Other Countries of the Former Soviet Union, by Donal McGettigan. 2000.

188. Financial Sector Crisis and Restructuring: Lessons from Asia, by Carl-Johan Lindgren, Tomás J.T. Baliño, Charles Enoch, Anne-Marie Gulde, Marc Quintyn, and Leslie Teo. 1999.

187. Philippines: Toward Sustainable and Rapid Growth, Recent Developments and the Agenda Ahead, by Markus Rodlauer, Prakash Loungani, Vivek Arora, Charalambos Christofides, Enrique G. De la Piedra, Piyabha Kongsamut, Kristina Kostial, Victoria Summers, and Athanasios Vamvakidis. 2000.

186. Anticipating Balance of Payments Crises: The Role of Early Warning Systems, by Andrew Berg, Eduardo Borensztein, Gian Maria Milesi-Ferretti, and Catherine Pattillo. 1999.

185. Oman Beyond the Oil Horizon: Policies Toward Sustainable Growth, edited by Ahsan Mansur and Volker Treichel. 1999.

184. Growth Experience in Transition Countries, 1990–98, by Oleh Havrylyshyn, Thomas Wolf, Julian Berengaut, Marta Castello-Branco, Ron van Rooden, and Valerie Mercer-Blackman. 1999.

183. Economic Reforms in Kazakhstan, Kyrgyz Republic, Tajikistan, Turkmenistan, and Uzbekistan, by Emine Gürgen, Harry Snoek, Jon Craig, Jimmy McHugh, Ivailo Izvorski, and Ron van Rooden. 1999.

182. Tax Reform in the Baltics, Russia, and Other Countries of the Former Soviet Union, by a Staff Team Led by Liam Ebrill and Oleh Havrylyshyn. 1999.

181. The Netherlands: Transforming a Market Economy, by C. Maxwell Watson, Bas B. Bakker, Jan Kees Martijn, and Ioannis Halikias. 1999.

180. Revenue Implications of Trade Liberalization, by Liam Ebrill, Janet Stotsky, and Reint Gropp. 1999.

179. Disinflation in Transition: 1993–97, by Carlo Cottarelli and Peter Doyle. 1999.

178. IMF-Supported Programs in Indonesia, Korea, and Thailand: A Preliminary Assessment, by Timothy Lane, Atish Ghosh, Javier Hamann, Steven Phillips, Marianne Schulze-Ghattas, and Tsidi Tsikata. 1999.

177. Perspectives on Regional Unemployment in Europe, by Paolo Mauro, Eswar Prasad, and Antonio Spilimbergo. 1999.

176. Back to the Future: Postwar Reconstruction and Stabilization in Lebanon, edited by Sena Eken and Thomas Helbling. 1999.

175. Macroeconomic Developments in the Baltics, Russia, and Other Countries of the Former Soviet Union, 1992–97, by Luis M. Valdivieso. 1998.

174. Impact of EMU on Selected Non–European Union Countries, by R. Feldman, K. Nashashibi, R. Nord, P. Allum, D. Desruelle, K. Enders, R. Kahn, and H. Temprano-Arroyo. 1998.

173. The Baltic Countries: From Economic Stabilization to EU Accession, by Julian Berengaut, Augusto Lopez-Claros, Françoise Le Gall, Dennis Jones, Richard Stern, Ann-Margret Westin, Effie Psalida, Pietro Garibaldi. 1998.

172. Capital Account Liberalization: Theoretical and Practical Aspects, by a staff team led by Barry Eichengreen and Michael Mussa, with Giovanni Dell'Ariccia, Enrica Detragiache, Gian Maria Milesi-Ferretti, and Andrew Tweedie. 1998.

171. Monetary Policy in Dollarized Economies, by Tomás Baliño, Adam Bennett, and Eduardo Borensztein. 1998.

170. The West African Economic and Monetary Union: Recent Developments and Policy Issues, by a staff team led by Ernesto Hernández-Catá and comprising Christian A. François, Paul Masson, Pascal Bouvier, Patrick Peroz, Dominique Desruelle, and Athanasios Vamvakidis. 1998.

169. Financial Sector Development in Sub-Saharan African Countries, by Hassanali Mehran, Piero Ugolini, Jean Phillipe Briffaux, George Iden, Tonny Lybek, Stephen Swaray, and Peter Hayward. 1998.

168. Exit Strategies: Policy Options for Countries Seeking Greater Exchange Rate Flexibility, by a staff team led by Barry Eichengreen and Paul Masson with Hugh Bredenkamp, Barry Johnston, Javier Hamann, Esteban Jadresic, and Inci Ötker. 1998.

167. Exchange Rate Assessment: Extensions of the Macroeconomic Balance Approach, edited by Peter Isard and Hamid Faruqee. 1998

166. Hedge Funds and Financial Market Dynamics, by a staff team led by Barry Eichengreen and Donald Mathieson with Bankim Chadha, Anne Jansen, Laura Kodres, and Sunil Sharma. 1998.

165. Algeria: Stabilization and Transition to the Market, by Karim Nashashibi, Patricia Alonso-Gamo, Stefania Bazzoni, Alain Féler, Nicole Laframboise, and Sebastian Paris Horvitz. 1998.

164. MULTIMOD Mark III: The Core Dynamic and Steady-State Model, by Douglas Laxton, Peter Isard, Hamid Faruqee, Eswar Prasad, and Bart Turtelboom. 1998.

163. Egypt: Beyond Stabilization, Toward a Dynamic Market Economy, by a staff team led by Howard Handy. 1998.

162. Fiscal Policy Rules, by George Kopits and Steven Symansky. 1998.

161. The Nordic Banking Crises: Pitfalls in Financial Liberalization? by Burkhard Dress and Ceyla Pazarbaşıoğlu. 1998.

160. Fiscal Reform in Low-Income Countries: Experience Under IMF-Supported Programs, by a staff team led by George T. Abed and comprising Liam Ebrill, Sanjeev Gupta, Benedict Clements, Ronald McMorran, Anthony Pellechio, Jerald Schiff, and Marijn Verhoeven. 1998.

159. Hungary: Economic Policies for Sustainable Growth, Carlo Cottarelli, Thomas Krueger, Reza Moghadam, Perry Perone, Edgardo Ruggiero, and Rachel van Elkan. 1998.

158. Transparency in Government Operations, by George Kopits and Jon Craig. 1998.

157. Central Bank Reforms in the Baltics, Russia, and the Other Countries of the Former Soviet Union, by a staff team led by Malcolm Knight and comprising Susana Almuiña, John Dalton, Inci Otker, Ceyla Pazarbaşıoğlu, Arne B. Petersen, Peter Quirk, Nicholas M. Roberts, Gabriel Sensenbrenner, and Jan Willem van der Vossen. 1997.

156. The ESAF at Ten Years: Economic Adjustment and Reform in Low-Income Countries, by the staff of the International Monetary Fund. 1997.

155. Fiscal Policy Issues During the Transition in Russia, by Augusto Lopez-Claros and Sergei V. Alexashenko. 1998.

154. Credibility Without Rules? Monetary Frameworks in the Post–Bretton Woods Era, by Carlo Cottarelli and Curzio Giannini. 1997.

153. Pension Regimes and Saving, by G.A. Mackenzie, Philip Gerson, and Alfredo Cuevas. 1997.

Note: For information on the title and availability of Occasional Papers not listed, please consult the IMF Publications Catalog or contact IMF Publication Services.